where to take
to take
Tea

$\frac{1}{7462}$

$\frac{1}{9218}$

$\frac{1}{7677}$

$\frac{1}{7004}$

$\frac{1}{9188}$

$\frac{1}{9243}$

$\frac{1}{8957}$

$\frac{1}{7578}$

where
to take
Tea

A guide to over 50 of the best places,

from Victorian tearooms to grand hotels

Susan Cohen

NEW HOLLAND

This book is dedicated to my mother, Edith, who loved Fullers' Iced Walnut Cake.

This paperback edition first published in 2008 by
New Holland Publishers (UK) Ltd
London • Cape Town • Sydney • Auckland

Garfield House
86–88 Edgware Road
London W2 2EA
www.newhollandpublishers.com

80 McKenzie Street
Cape Town 8001
South Africa

Unit 1
66 Gibbes Street
Chatswood, NSW 2067
Australia

218 Lake Road
Northcote
Auckland
New Zealand

1 3 5 7 9 10 8 6 4 2

ISBN 978 1 84537 987 2

Senior Editor: Clare Hubbard
Original Design: Cube
Design Modifications for Paperback: Casebourne Rose Design Associates
Editorial Direction: Rosemary Wilkinson
Production: Hazel Kirkman

Reproduction by Modern Age Repro, Hong Kong
Printed and bound by Times Offset (M) Sdn Bhd, Malaysia

Contents

Author's Foreword

UPDATING this book has been just as pleasurable as writing the first edition was some five years ago. Some of the places I included then, especially out of London, have closed down or have changed hands, so this edition includes new entries as well as many of the original ones. Friends and family often ask me how I came to write it, given that my time is usually divided between working as an interior decorator and undertaking academic historical research. In all honesty, it came about by accident rather than design, but can be blamed on my love of social history, a chance encounter with some fascinating teashop archives and my enjoyment of scones and afternoon tea. The outcome was this nostalgic, illustrated social history of tea and a guide to 50 of the best tea venues in Britain, from fine hotels to cosy teashops.

Thanks are due to Amy Corbett at New Holland, who helped with all the changes that needed to be made. To all the lovely people whose tea I have tasted and whose scones I have eaten, a big thank you. Regular walking with good friends has helped me keep the extra pounds at bay – except when we finish our trek with a traditional afternoon tea of scones and jam!

Lastly, I hope that you gain as much enjoyment from reading the book as I have from compiling it.

Introduction

If you are cold, tea will warm you –
If you are too heated, it will cool you –
If you are depressed, it will cheer you –
If you are excited, it will calm you.

MR WILLIAM E. GLADSTONE
BRITISH PRIME MINISTER (1809–98)

QUEEN Victoria's Prime Minister, William Gladstone, captured the very essence of tea when he wrote these words in 1865. Relaxing, refreshing, stimulating or warming, there is little to compare with the comfort and delights of a steaming pot of tea. There is a certain magical, even mystical quality about tea, not least of all because of the amazing influence the tiny leaf exerts on everyday life. A cup of tea is the best reason in the world to stop for a break during the day. Life's rites of passage would not be the same without tea, and the variety of leaves is such that every mood and taste can be catered for. As the world's most popular drink, tea crosses all the boundaries of history, nation, culture and class. At some time in their lives, most people, even the smallest child, acquire a "taste" for tea, a habit that they rarely relinquish. Whilst the paraphernalia and rituals surrounding tea have a tantalizing effect on collectors, connoisseurs and the merely inquisitive, the social aspects of tea-drinking are fascinating and evocative of leisure and pleasure. Why not relax with a cup of tea whilst you read on…

William Gladstone's eulogy on tea (above left) was paired with this illustration and made into a postcard.

the
story of
Tea

Tea has a fascinating history. Its story is intertwined with social trends and political events throughout the world, from the Japanese tea ceremony to the Boston Tea Party. Throughout its history it has been at the centre of people's lives, whether for comfort during wartime, as a partner to the tango or simple refreshment at a welcoming tearoom.

How it All Began

Where better to begin than with an introduction to the fascinating story of how tea-drinking began in the East and then travelled to the West.

Origins in the Orient

THE story of tea-drinking began, as legend has it, as long ago as 2737 B.C., when the Chinese Emperor, Shen Nung, accidentally discovered the delights of camellia leaves – a relative of the tea leaf – steeped in hot water. However, centuries passed before the Chinese took to grinding up the leaves and whisking them in hot water or making flat cakes from them. The era of the Ming Dynasty, between 1368 and 1644, seems to have been a turning point in the history of tea-drinking, for it was during these years that the more familiar method of brewing leaves in hot water became a favourite pastime. The Oriental influence on tea

Japanese Tea Ceremony

The basis of the modern tea ceremony was established by Murato Shuko (1422–1502), renowned for his design of the 3-metre square (9-foot square) Japanese tearoom. He was the first person to make tea in front of his guests. At the heart of the tea ceremony are the four principles of wa-kei-sei-jaku, – harmony, respect, purity and tranquillity.

grew once the beverage travelled from China to Japan, for the Japanese turned tea-drinking into a celebration and honoured it with an elaborate ceremony.

Britain and Tea

WHEN tea was first introduced into Britain, it was known by its Cantonese name, *ch'a*, but after Britain's trading base was moved from Canton to Amoy (Fujian Province, China) at the end of the seventeenth century, the drink acquired a new and more familiar name, *tay* and later *tee*.

The British upper classes got their first taste of tea in around 1645, when the East India Trading Company introduced it to the country. Britain's monopoly on the export of the leaf meant that it was an expensive and scarce commodity, made even more so by the 119 per cent tax rate imposed by King Charles II's parliament. Very few ordinary people could afford to buy the leaf but this suited a number of groups – brewers, church leaders and medical men – very well. The brewers feared that "the meanest families, even the labouring people in Scotland [would] make their morning meal of tea to the disuse of ale". Leaders of the Church of England treated the Eastern provenance of tea with suspicion and concluded that it led to sin, whilst doctors – who actually knew very

This set of three silver tea caddies in a contemporary case date back to 1739.

little about medicine at this time – were certain that tea made people ill.

Scarcity and price made tea the ultimate status symbol and a fashionable luxury. It was given the royal seal of approval by Catherine of Braganza, the Portuguese wife of King Charles II, as she brought a chest of tea with her as part of her dowry in 1662. Little did she know how much solace she would find in her cup of tea, which she sipped whilst her husband frolicked with his favourite mistress, Nell Gwyn. Meanwhile, tea smugglers did a roaring trade and rich ladies became so protective of the luxury leaf that they kept it under lock and key in a stylish tea caddy – perhaps made by the celebrated English cabinetmaker, Thomas Chippendale (1718–79). Unlocking the caddy was as much a part of the ritual of

> 66 *Strong tea and scandal –*
> *Bless me how refreshing.* 99

THE SCHOOL FOR SCANDAL *1777*
THE FAMOUS PLAYWRIGHT, RICHARD BRINSLEY
SHERIDAN, MIGHT WELL HAVE WRITTEN THESE
WORDS FOR QUEEN CATHERINE.

serving tea to their guests as were the frivolous diversions of cards and music.

The tea scene in Britain changed dramatically because of events in America in 1773. History recalls how the colonial population, tired of the tax on tea, took it upon themselves to break the East India Company's long monopoly. Bedecked in native Indian outfits, large crowds unceremoniously dumped the tea cargo into Boston harbour in protest at the company's profiteering. The Boston Tea Party, as it became known, was one of the events that led to the American War of Independence.

Tea cargo being dumped into Boston harbour.

However, the most radical change to tea-drinking habits in Britain occurred in 1784 when William Pitt (1759–1806), then Prime Minister of Britain, finally reduced Chancellor of the Exchequer Cromwell's tax on tea to 12 per cent, making the beverage affordable by rich and poor alike. Tea became the drink of the masses.

Buying and Selling Tea

ONE of the first people to realize the potential of buying and selling tea was Thomas Garway, the owner of Garraway's Coffee House in Cornhill, in the City of London. He organized the earliest recorded London tea auction, in Mincing Lane in 1657. The following year the unnamed owner of another coffee house, The Sultaness Head, placed an advertisement in a popular news sheet offering "China *Tcha, Tay* or *Tee*" for sale. Until 1826 tea was always sold loose, by weight, but John Horniman, a merchant on the Isle of Wight, changed this when he had the novel idea of selling small quantities of leaf tea made up in labelled packets.

The Victorians owed a huge debt to Thomas Lipton, an entrepreneur who learnt the ins and outs of the tea trade in America before opening up his first shop selling tea in Glasgow in 1871. By 1900 his empire had grown to 100 shops and he was selling a million packs of the exotic commodity annually. Affordable tea was now widely available across Britain, with the "Lipton" name associated with tea throughout the world.

It was not only hot tea that became a firm favourite. In hot climates iced tea makes a very refreshing drink, as tea merchant Richard Blechynden discovered at the World's Fair in St Louis, America in 1904. During the heat wave no one was interested in trying his hot tea. Desperate to attract customers, he took a chance and added ice to the brew and was overwhelmed by the success of his newly-invented drink – iced tea.

Tea Innovations

In the early 1900s, an American travelling salesman, Thomas Sullivan, put small amounts of tea in silk drawstring bags so he could provide his customers with samples of his wares – and so the tea bag was born.

Tea Races and Tea-clippers

TRANSPORTING tea from China to London was a costly and time-consuming business and led to intense rivalry between ship owners, each eager to lead the field. The tea-clipper, a sleek, tall ship built for speed but large and strong enough to carry huge amounts of cargo, proved to be the early key to success, replacing the older frigate-built ships known jokingly as "tea-waggons". A clipper could reach speeds of up to 18 knots, even when it was carrying a typical tea cargo weighing approximately 454,000 kilograms (450 tons). In 1845 an

A nineteenth-century tea-clipper on the high seas.

American clipper smashed the 15-month journey time set by the East India Company and made the round trip from New York in less than eight months. Not to be beaten, the British built their own fleet of fast ships, including the most famous of all, the Cutty Sark. It is now in dry dock in Greenwich and can be visited.

Before long tea races became a popular sport, much to the delight of gamblers. In London bets were placed on the results of races, whilst the captain of the winning vessel stood to win a large bonus. The most celebrated tea race took place in mid-1866 when three of the forty competing vessels docked simultaneously in London, having made the journey from China in just 99 days.

> ### The Chaa-sze
> *There was no mistaking the cargo of one particular British clipper, the Chaa-sze (Tea-taster), for it had a figurehead of a Chinese man and included representations of tea chests, teapots, cups and saucers.*

The heyday of the tea-clipper was short lived. By 1870, the year after the Suez Canal was opened, they had been replaced by the revolutionary steamships which plied their way across the oceans, reducing the transport time by weeks.

Reading the Leaves

MANY people – especially those who could not afford a mote spoon (used for scooping loose leaf tea from the caddy to the teapot and skimming leaves from the surface of the tea once it had been poured into the cup) or a silver tea strainer – put great store in the power of the leaves which were left at the bottom of their cup, certain that when "read" they would reveal future events.

> " Matrons who toss the cup, and see
> The grounds of fate in grounds of tea. "
>
> ALEXANDER POPE (N.D)

Postcard entitled *Stranger in the Teacup*.

The Power of the Leaves

Some pictures to look out for in the tea leaves at the bottom of your cup:

Anchor *A voyage*
Arrow *Bad news*
Bird *Good news or travel by air*
Cat *Good luck*
Circle *Trust and love*
Crescent moon *Changes*
Devil *Unbridled passions*
Dog *Good friends*
Door *An unusual event*
Eagle *Strength, overcoming adversity*
Egg *Increase*
Eye *Understanding*
Fairy *Romance*
Feather *Lack of concentration*
Fire *Impetuousness*
Fish *Fertility*
Flower *Happiness and success*
Geese *Sign of unwelcome visitors*
Heart *Love*
Iceberg *Hidden dangers*
Kite *Lofty ambitions*
Ladder *Advancement*
Mouth *Listen carefully*
Nest *Security*
Peacock *Immortality*
Pirate *Adventure*
Rainbow *Future good luck*
Ring *Marriage*
Sun *Warmth and happiness*
Tree *Recovery after an illness*
Vulture *Theft*

Tea and Health

DEVOTEES of tea never doubted that tea revived and refreshed and early advocates promoted it as a panacea for all ills, including headaches, weariness, colds, scurvy, dropsy and an unpleasant-sounding condition called "liptude distillations". In 1667 claims were made that tea was an effective treatment for gout. The first printed advertisement for tea appeared in 1669, by courtesy of Thomas Garway, the owner of the well-known London Coffee House, Garraways. He maintained that tea "would not only make the body active and lusty" but that it would "removeth the obstructions of the spleen". In recent years there has been much research into the health benefits of tea and many of the claims made hundreds of years ago have in fact been proved to be true.

> *Peter was not very well during the evening. His mother put him to bed, and made some chamomile tea: "One tablespoonful to be taken at bed-time."*

PETER RABBIT BEATRIX POTTER

Tea Paraphernalia

TEA'S new found popularity was a blessing for entrepreneurs and craftsmen, for it created a huge industry of tea-related paraphernalia. From china to silver, linen to lace, everything that was produced reflected the fashions of the day.

One of the first people in Britain to take advantage of the manufacturing

> *Throughout the whole of England the drinking of tea is general. You have it twice a day and though the expense is considerable, the humblest peasant has his tea, just like the rich man.*

LA ROCHEFOUCAULD, 1784

opportunities was Josiah Wedgwood, a shrewd businessman and pioneering potter. In 1765 he was commissioned to make a tea and coffee service for Queen Charlotte, wife of the tea devotee King George III. The Queen was so delighted with this special cream ware set that she gave Royal Assent for Wedgwood to call the design "Queen's Ware".

Queen's Ware teapot and hot-water jug, circa 1765–70, showing traces of gilding in the moulding, most of which has been worn away.

Hot on Wedgwood's heels was Josiah Spode who, by 1815, had perfected the formula for making fine bone china. The brilliant whiteness and translucent beauty of Spode bone china so captivated the Prince of Wales that he later granted the company the first of their six royal

This section of a page from a 1900 Copeland catalogue shows the wide variety of cup shapes which were available to Victorian shoppers.

warrants. Europe had its own master craftsmen – factories at Meissen in Germany and Sèvres in France produced exquisite teasets that were hand-painted and often elaborately gilded.

Before long hostesses were demanding matching sets of tea-ware – not just the *de rigueur* teapot and mote spoon or tea strainer, but also a slop bowl to pour the dregs into, a sugar bowl with tongs, a milk jug and creamer and a teaspoon to stir with. Only later, during the Victorian era, did the tea cosy, cake-stand, bread and butter plate, tea knife, and cake and pastry forks become essential and fashionable items on the tea-table.

The ships that brought tea from China also carried tea-ware items, so it was not surprising that the Orient inspired the earliest European designs for teacups and saucers. But the Chinese practice of sipping hot tea from tea bowls – small cups without handles – was too much for the sensitive hands of British ladies. Manufacturers such as Spode and Wedgwood soon came up with a solution and created an innovative and more practical style of cup, which incorporated a handle, thus preventing delicate hands getting burnt.

However, tea was not always drunk from the cup. Saucers were added toward the end of the eighteenth century and were often used to cover the cup of tea while it infused. The tea was then poured into the saucer to be drunk.

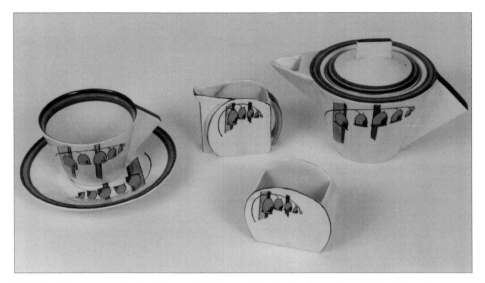

Part of the Bizarre ware collection, Solomon's Seal has a printed floral outline coloured in lilac, blue and green.

Fashions came and went and with them the shape of cups and handles changed. When Art Deco was the rage in the 1920s, Clarice Cliff (1899-1972), the celebrated English ceramic designer, created a range that was as unusual as its name. Made from earthenware, Bizarre's bold geometric design and continental shape captivated the public, only to be surpassed in popularity by Cliff's 1929 Conical Range with its solid triangular handles.

Teapots

...here was a table set out under a tree in front of the house, and the March Hare and the Hatter were having tea at it: ... the last time she saw them, they were trying to put the Dormouse into the teapot. "At any rate I'll never go there again!" said Alice..."

ALICE'S ADVENTURES IN WONDERLAND
LEWIS CARROLL

Too Hot to Handle

The Duchess of Lauderdale regretted her purchase of a set of silver teacups in 1672, for they were impossible to use as the handles became unbearably hot.

THE first teapots to be imported into Europe from China were tiny, their size reflecting the high cost of tea. Wedgwood and Spode created delicate and highly decorated teapots whilst other manufacturers responded to current trends, producing novelty teapots in various shapes or caricatures of public figures. Silversmiths

How it All Began | 17

created tea-services that were both works of art, well suited to grace the homes of the rich and famous, and also items to be treasured as family heirlooms. Collecting was a fashion started by King George IV whilst he was the Prince Regent.

A magnificently worked Spode teapot in the Imari style with an abundance of gold, cobalt blue, emerald green and old scarlet from 1811. Pattern 1645.

The advent of electricity heralded a new adventure in tea-making. "Boiling the kettle" no longer meant having a kettle hanging over an open fire as the electric kettle became commonplace in the home. A more extraordinary invention for tea devotees was the automatic tea-maker, a machine that looked as if it would be more at home in one of W. Heath Robinson's comic illustrations.

The Tea Leaf

IMAGINE rolling hills in the tropics and sub-tropics and vast expanses of green shrubs, neatly pruned into level planes and one gets an idea of the plantations where the tea plant, *Thea Sinensis,* a member of the Camellia family, is grown. Altitude, temperature and rainfall are crucial elements in the tea-producing equation and each affects the quality of the end product. Even though there are more than 2,000 different varieties of tea, an experienced taster can identify the region, even the slope that a particular leaf was grown on and can detect how much rain fell the day the leaf was picked. In any one day a tea buyer may work their way through 400 samples, sipping it from a silver spoon to check, amongst other qualities, its "briskness" (how long the taste lingers in the mouth). The finest tea leaves are the young tender ones and in keeping with tradition, are generally still handpicked by women. The job is far from easy, particularly when one considers that the most superior leaves are grown at altitudes of 900–1,800 metres (3,000–6,000 feet) above sea-level. For the best results, freshly plucked leaves must be sent immediately for processing.

The tenderest top two leaves and bud are used in the highest grades of teas.

Growing tea bushes, following the natural contours of the lush landscape.

66 I pray thee, gentle Renny dear,
That thou will give to me,
With cream and sugar temper'd well,
Another dish of tea.

Nor fear that I, my gentle maid,
Shall long detain the cup,
When once unto the bottom I
Have drank the liquor up.

Yet hear, at last, this mournful truth,
Nor hear it with a frown,
Thou canst not make the tea so fast,
As I can gulp it down. 99

SAMUEL JOHNSON, TAKEN FROM
LIFE OF JOHNSON SIR JOHN HAWKINS

Types of Tea

THERE are six types of tea – black, green, white, oolong, scented and compressed.

Black tea includes Assam, Darjeeling and Nilgiri from India, Ceylon from Sri Lanka and Keemun and Lapsang Souchong from China – each of which has its own distinctive flavour and aroma. It is produced after the leaves have undergone four processing stages – withering (which happens when the leaves are laid out to dry), rolling, fermenting (a process which makes the leaves turn their familiar brownish colour and imparts a healthy flavour) and drying. Darjeeling – considered to be the champagne of teas – is grown at varying altitudes in the Himalayas and the higher up it is grown, the lighter the tea. Especially prized by connoisseurs is the new season's tea, the light and fragrant first flush Darjeeling, picked in April.

Oolong tea is semi-fermented and is generally the most expensive type of tea. The best varieties are produced in Taiwan and include the exclusive Monkey Picked.

Green tea, which is paler and milder than black tea, was the first to be enjoyed throughout the world, but its popularity waned as people showed a preference for a stronger brew. There are only two processing stages involved in producing green tea; rolling and drying. Varieties include Gunpowder from China and Matcha and Sencha from Japan.

White tea is produced in very small quantities in China and Sri Lanka and is available from specialist tea suppliers. A tea for the connoisseur.

Compressed teas are formed into ball, brick, nest and cake shapes. These are produced in China.

Scented teas are made from green, oolong or black teas flavoured with fruits, herbs, spices and flowers, such as roses, orchids and jasmine.

Blended teas have an important place in modern tea-drinking, particularly the English Breakfast tea blend. Originally a mix of black Indian and China teas, nowadays Assam, Ceylon and African teas are blended to provide drinkers with the three elements they require – strength, flavour and colour. More exotic sounding is Russian Caravan tea – named after the camel caravan that brought China tea to Europe along the silk and spice trade route – a blend of China tea. Earl Grey, so-called after Charles, Second Earl Grey who was the Prime Minister of Britain between 1830 and 1834, is a popular blend. Made with Indian and China teas, flavoured with bergamot oil, it is a refreshing tea, best served black or with lemon.

One Spoon or Two?

THE basic rules which most people follow today include using freshly drawn and boiled water and allowing one teaspoonful of loose leaf tea or one tea bag per person. Brewing time is, it is agreed, all-important and depends on the type of tea you are brewing. Darjeeling requires from 3 to 5 minutes, Kenya from 2 to 4 minutes and China Oolong 5 to 7 minutes. However, at what point you add milk has been a contentious subject for decades. Victorian

etiquette was definite on this matter: the milk or cream (a teaset always included a cream jug) had to be put in last, so that its addition could be rejected or limited. The British novelist and essayist, George Orwell (1903–1950), who published his own 11 golden rules for a "nice cup of tea" in 1945, had equally firm views. Last was best, he wrote, for "by putting the tea in first and then stirring as one pours, one can exactly regulate the amount of milk". The last word could go to Nancy Mitford, the English aristocrat novelist and biographer, who claimed that "milk in first", known as the "MIF" debate, was without doubt, not the "thing" to do.

Tea and Temperance

66 *The domestic use of tea is a powerful champion able to encounter alcoholic drink in a fair field and throw it in a fair fight.* 99

PRIME MINISTER GLADSTONE IN HIS BUDGET SPEECH OF 1882

PRIME Minister Gladstone was not the only Victorian to advocate tea-drinking, for the beverage was a boon to the Temperance Movement in their fight against the demon "drink". In cities like Liverpool, Birmingham and Preston, tea meetings were held which attracted as many as 2,500 people. Unsurprisingly, tea featured on the "menu" along with "singing, recitation and dialogue" – all intended to persuade folk to give up intoxicating liquor.

Tea Rationing

TEA has a reputation for being the national drink of Britain and at no time was its popularity greater than in wartime, when its restorative powers were so badly needed. It's hard to imagine now the effect that tea rationing had on a nation at war. But for 12 years, between 1940 and 1952, the government took charge of all tea imports, allocating it to dealers who then distributed it to shoppers. During this time the amount that each person was allowed per week varied between 50–75 grammes (2–2½ ounces) and there must have been a great sigh of relief in homes up and down the land when rationing finally came to an end in 1952.

Punch magazine captured the British weakness for tea in this wartime cartoon, entitled *War Time Weaknesses – Cups of Tea.*

A cup of tea was welcomed by these two youngsters who were evacuated from London in June 1940. It made them feel at home in strange surroundings.

Outdoor and Travelling Tea

Since the early eighteenth century, tea has been a favourite drink to be enjoyed in all situations – tea gardens and parties, picnic teas and travelling teas.

Tea Gardens

THERE were more than 500 coffee houses selling tea by 1700, but by 1730 these all-male establishments had fallen out of favour and become the haunts of scoundrels and villains. High society – which included ladies – had now found a more salubrious way of enjoying afternoon tea in the new tea gardens which had sprung up, especially in the metropolis.

Between 1732 and about 1852, tea gardens including Vauxhall in South London, Marylebone, Ranelagh in Chelsea and Bagnigge Wells, east of London's Grays Inn Road, were the places where fashionable Georgians went to see and be seen. At Ranelagh they could expect to be served with "fine Imperial tea and other delicious refreshments" whilst at Vauxhall they could enjoy the beauty of a most enchanting lily garden.

Bagnigge Wells Tea Garden in 1778. The centre of the garden had a small round fishpond, in the midst of which was a curious fountain representing a Cupid astride a swan. Water spouted out of the swan's beak at a great height, much to the delight of onlookers.

> *Old Vauxhall Gardens must have been a charming place for flirtations, for the windings and turnings in the wildernesses were so intricate that the most experienced mothers often lost themselves in looking for their daughters.*
>
> HIGHWAYS AND BYWAYS IN LONDON,
> E. COOK (1902)

Harmony and music were the great traditions of the Marylebone Tea Garden and the composer Handel regularly visited to listen to his cantatas being performed. A less welcome visitor was the burly Duke of Cumberland (1721–1765) who was renowned for disturbing the peaceful atmosphere by his rude behaviour. Bagnigge Wells was regarded by the ladies as "the last word of modish resort". A contemporary writer described the gardens: "... laid out with clipped hedges of yew, the formal walks edged by box and holly and the arbours covered with sweetbrier and honeysuckle for tea drinking".

At night the walkways of the tea gardens were illuminated by lanterns, transforming the ornately landscaped gardens into entrancing, magical places. Ordinary folk soon adopted the tea garden idea and more modest venues opened up, offering the working classes, who were thrilled at the opportunity of a day out, a value-for-money excursion.

Visitors of all classes could spend their time watching events from the shelter of stylish, well-furnished arbours and the entertainment – musicians, fireworks, acrobats, jugglers and magicians – was lavish. The entrance fee, which always included the unlimited "regale" of tea,

coffee and bread and butter, varied from place to place and time of day. An entirely different type of tea garden had emerged by the 1930s, in locations such as Kew Gardens and Hyde Park. Here visitors could enjoy a pot of tea at a table under an umbrella for less than half the price charged at the grander tea gardens.

Tea-garden Parties

FROM the moment that Queen Victoria held her first royal tea party at Buckingham Palace in 1868, the idea of the tea-garden party became a popular, fashionable and very English entertainment. The royal connection enhanced the reputation of

Photographed in 1951 in the grounds of Buckingham Palace, Queen Elizabeth, the Queen Mother was fond of the Nippys, who regularly served at her London garden parties. On this occasion the Nippys were not wearing their starched white coronet caps – perhaps they didn't want to be seen to be competing with royalty.

Ridgway's, the tea importers, for they were invited to create a special blend for Queen Victoria. This blend was then served at garden parties, alongside the finger sandwiches and pastries. Just how regular the royal garden parties were before 1948 is difficult to say, but between 1948 and 1958 the monarch was "at home" in London to specially invited guests on two afternoons in July – and on one such occasion whilst in summer residence at the Palace of Holyrood House, in Edinburgh. Garden parties are still a regular event at Buckingham Palace. For many years J. Lyons and Co. were the official caterers and the famous Nippy waitress was to be seen on the lawns of Buckingham Palace (see page 40).

Afternoon Tea

UP until the 1840s tea was only drunk at breakfast or after dinner as a digestif, but once again the aristocracy played its part in changing fashion. For it was Anna Maria, the Seventh Duchess of Bedford, who is popularly credited with introducing the idea of afternoon tea. By all accounts she suffered from such gnawing hunger pains in the long gap between lunch and dinner at 9 o'clock, that she ordered her maid to serve tea and cakes at 5 o'clock to alleviate these "sinking feelings". This was the start of the formal afternoon tea.

The Tea Break and High Tea

A different gap was filled by the tea break which was introduced more than 200 years ago. Labourers and rural workers were served tea and food mid-morning and late afternoon to tide them over until they returned home for their evening meal. For many workers, afternoon tea was replaced by high tea, an end-of-working-day meal which combined tea and early supper. This tradition still lingers on, particularly in the north of England and Scotland. Hearty hot and cold food is served alongside cakes, bread, butter and jam and the not-to-be forgotten pot of steaming tea, with all its restorative powers.

These London and North Eastern Railway workers are being served tea by a tealady in the workshops at Temple Mills, watched closely by their supervisor. This photograph was taken in July 1941.

Tea Picnics

WITH the public taste for taking tea out-of-doors well established, a new idea, that of the tea picnic, evolved. Victorian and Edwardian society were particularly partial to these outings, so much so that Mrs Beeton (1836–65), the Victorian authority on cookery and domestic science, whose

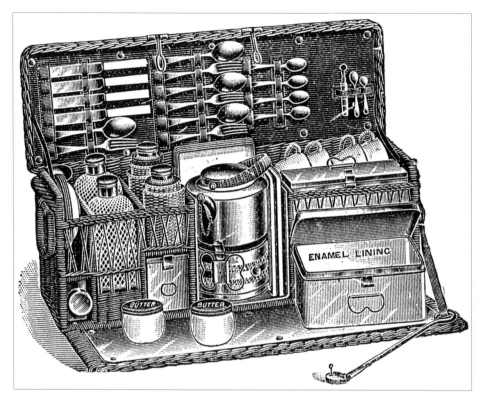

This tea basket was one of a dozen or more designs available to the discerning Harrods shopper in 1912.

renowned *Book on Household Management* was first published in 1861, included picnic menus in her publications. Tea was clearly an essential part of the ritual, for she advised that "A kettle and teapot must be taken if they cannot be borrowed; nor should a box of matches, a little dry wood and a cloth for wiping cups be forgotten". Society events and the "season", which included horse-racing at Ascot and Epsom, boating at Henley Royal Regatta, cricket at Lord's, opera at Glyndbourne and tennis at Wimbledon, provided followers of fashion with the ideal opportunity of enjoying a lavish tea picnic.

In fact it seems that visitors often took more interest in the traditional serving of tea than the event itself. Tables and chairs would be set out with crisp, fresh linen cloths and neatly folded napkins and the full range of tea-ware – including silver teapot and hot-water jug – would appear. There was no problem in safely transporting all the paraphernalia because specially designed tea-picnic baskets had been introduced by the most renowned department stores, for just such occasions. The invention of the Thermos flask in 1904 enabled Edwardian travellers to keep their drinks piping hot.

However you travelled there was always a cup of tea around the corner, as these cyclists in Cotesbach, Leicestershire discovered in 1935.

Travelling Tea

TEA was such an important part of everyday life for the Victorians that it rapidly became available wherever they went. This was the golden age of the railways and the train companies quickly saw the potential for extra profit by satisfying the thirsty passengers. The first railway buffet to serve tea was opened by the catering company, Spiers and Pond, on Farringdon Station, London, in 1866. The fully-equipped tea trolley – including the near-indestructible aspidistra plant, so beloved of the Victorians – made its first appearance on the platforms of main-line stations and liveried staff served a wide selection of refreshments to waiting passengers.

Alternatively, travellers could purchase a specially-fitted tea basket to take with them on their journey. Day or night, staff were on hand when trains arrived at stations, ready to deliver the complete kit. The Great Western Railways basket had an enamelled-iron lining and contained hot water, milk, sugar, three slices of bread and butter, cake and a piece of fresh fruit.

First-class passengers could, if they preferred, have afternoon tea served on board the train. In the comfort of their private compartment, perhaps on their way to connect with an Atlantic liner docked in Liverpool, a Victorian lady would partake of toasted teacakes, assorted sandwiches and cakes, alongside the pot of Indian or

China tea. But, as the Great Western Railway were to discover years later, the cost of serving cups of tea on the trains was unexpectedly expensive. For just before the outbreak of the Second World War, the company reported that they lost an astonishing 240,000 of their specially stamped cups every year. Some certainly turned up in the soldiers' kit, but where the rest went to remains a mystery.

When the motorcar became the latest mode of travel, drivers and their entourage had no difficulty in obtaining a cup of tea during their journey, especially in the south of England. Apart from the roadside café, the 1930s holidaymaker could rely upon the tea caravan – a caravan drawn by a small motorcar – which was located at popular roadside spots, serving holidaymakers with tea and cakes.

Tea at the Cinema

No afternoon visit to the cinema in the 1930s and 1940s was complete without a cup of tea. Patrons could order a tray of tea to be brought to them in their seats during the intermission. If you visited one of the "super" cinemas – one of the larger, more elaborate venues which sprang up everywhere after 1929 – you could enjoy a pot of the beverage in the cinema café, to the accompaniment of a Palm Court orchestra.

Imagine the thrill for the really adventurous tea-loving traveller, when in 1927, during the months of May to October, the Imperial Airways Company ran regular afternoon flights over the City of London and served a first class tea.

The aircraft used for the afternoon flights over the City of London was the Armstrong Whitworth Argosy. Passengers would get a wonderful view of the metropolis whilst...

...drinking their tea and sampling delicious food in less-than-spacious conditions.

——— *Tea and Symphony* ———

This is the story of how dancing and afternoon tea combined to become a fashionable and popular form of entertainment and how the tango started it all.

Tea-dancing

66 *What could be pleasanter, for instance,
on a dull wintry afternoon,
at five o'clock or so, when calls or shopping
are over, than to drop in
to one of the cheery little "Thé Dansant"
clubs, which have sprung up
all over the West End...to take one's place
at a tiny table...to enjoy a
most elaborate and delicious tea...whilst
listening to an excellent string
band (and)...joining in the dance...* 99

MRS GLADYS CROZIER, 1913

WHEN Mrs Gladys Crozier, society hostess and leading authority on tea-dancing, wrote these words in her authoritative book on the subject in 1913, little did she know how popular this form of entertainment would become. Some of London's elite had toyed with the idea of a "dancing" tea in 1845, much to the amusement of the recently launched, humorous satirical journal *Punch*. On the other hand, continental society was already well accustomed to the afternoon diversion, for fashionable Moroccans regularly danced a gentle valse around the afternoon tea-table. Similarly tea-dancing had already caught on in the best Parisian drawing-rooms. But,

what started out as a respectable, harmless diversion in France, was soon transformed into a daring and risqué spectacle, all due to the arrival of the very provocative Argentine tango on French dance floors around 1912.

> ### The Origins of Tango
> *Gladys Crozier gave two explanations for the word "tango". One said it was derived from* tangonette, *the name of a special kind of castanet, the other from the verb* tangir, *to touch.*
> (*The Times Literary Supplement, 18 December 1913*)

Suddenly "tango teas" became the rage of high society. The high-class dress-designer Lady Duff Gordon – otherwise known by her professional name of Madame Lucile – recalled how everyone in Paris was "tango-mad" before the First World War, "from *la haute société* down to the little *midinettes* who could be seen practising new steps in the Jardin des Tuileries in their lunch-hour." Parisians, who were known to be daring and trend-setting, had never seen anything to compare with the sensuous

An amusing satirical view of the tea dance entitled *Thé Dansante*, in an 1845 edition of *Punch*, which had more to do with balancing skills than dancing talent.

tango. Nor had Kaiser Wilhelm of Germany, who had banned the dance because he thought it totally decadent and only Bohemian café society in Argentina dared to dance it. From capital to coast, the tango tea became the most popular pastime amongst high society. Sophisticated socialites in the fashionable resorts of Deauville and Dinard were guaranteed an afternoon's tango tea at the casino or any of the best hotels. In Lucerne, the elite establishments vied for clients to tango at teatime; and not to be left out, the dance got Ostend "...by the throat". Returning to British shores, the dance crossed the high seas and by 1913 tango teas were making headline news in London and being advertised in many of the popular papers.

> ## Tango Lessons
> *Fortunes were made from dancing lessons in Paris. In 1913,* The Daily Mail *reported that a Parisian instructor was working from breakfast-time to late in the evening, giving half-hour long tango classes to groups of two or three pupils in the Place Vendome, and charging each person £12. Put into context; in Britain in 1912, the average annual income was £80.*

Tango teas at the Prince's Restaurant in Piccadilly were one of the social highlights of late 1913. Every day a wide central space was cleared and all the tables gathered around so that guests had a bird's eye view of the professional dancing demonstration.

The Place to be Seen

LIKE the rush for tea-ware a century before, "tangomania" led to an explosion of golden opportunities for entrepreneurs. From people hurrying to open tea-dance clubs, to dressmakers, milliners and cobblers frantically trying to produce suitable dresses, hats and shoes, to teachers vying to give lessons, the atmosphere was quite feverish in Edwardian London. Amongst the most enthusiastic were the new generation of tea-dancers, who suddenly found themselves freed from the strict constraints of Victorian society. After all, what danger could there be in young men and women meeting, unchaperoned, in public in the afternoon, to share the pleasure of a cup of tea and a dance?

Amongst the most select tea-dance clubs to open in the metropolis were the "Four Hundred Club" in Old Bond Street, the Carlton Hotel, the Thé Tango Club at Prince's Restaurant and the Boston Club at the Grafton Gallery. The "Four Hundred Club" included "Royalty, an English Duke or two, many well-known peers and some of the most shining lights of the musical-comedy stage" amongst its members.

But of all the tea-dance venues in London, there was nowhere that could compare with the Savoy. The tea-dance experience at the Savoy was the ultimate in good taste, style and sophistication. The tea-tables were beautifully set with the hotel's hallmark pink tablecloths, *le thé Russe* was prepared by a Russian expert and menus were presented in French to preserve the continental feel so loved by high society. A magnificent new rising ballroom floor was installed in the restaurant foyer in 1928, much to the chagrin of their envious competitors. Patrons enjoying a tango tea at the Savoy in the 1920s were serenaded by the first genuine tango band to play in the country. And in November 1933, teatime visitors were the first to see a new dance, the Charleston Blues, demonstrated on the Savoy dance floor by the champion ballroom dancer, Victor Silvester.

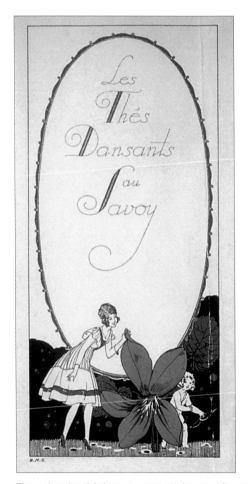

These charming *thé dansant* menus set the scene for a totally indulgent afternoon tea at The Savoy.

Victor Silvester

Victor Silvester's ballroom dancing career only started after a chance meeting with the well-known teacher Miss Belle Harding over the teacups and tango in Harrods Georgian Restaurant in 1919.

As the tango craze gained momentum, expert tuition became a must and many teachers combined lessons with a tea dance. A Miss Lennard was in attendance at the select tea dance at the Waldorf Hotel, whilst Miss Belle Harding, presided over *thé tangos* at the Hotel Cecil and the Royal Palace Hotel Kensington – that was when she was not gallivanting around organizing *thé dansant* and tango teas the length and breadth of the country. These out-of-town events were so popular that hundreds of would-be dancers were apparently turned away from venues each week.

Even though the tango was modified to make it more acceptable and respectable, many Edwardians expressed outrage and the popular press was littered with anti-tango letters denouncing the dance as "indecent, scandalous and obscene".

Maurice and Leonora Hughes were the exhibition dancers at this *thé dansant* held in the restaurant foyer of the Savoy Hotel in October 1920. The band playing that day were Sherbo's Orchestra, a five-piece American band.

Frocks Galore

THE fashion for afternoon tea breathed new life into late-Victorian and Edwardian dress design, for the tight-waisted and bustled dresses of the day left little room for sandwiches and cakes, however dainty they were. By the 1880s, the Dress Reform Society were already encouraging women to wear less restrictive and harmful clothing and a more relaxed style of garment began to emerge, much to the delight of the couture dressmaker. To be thoroughly fashionable the hostess who was entertaining at home wore one of the new tea gowns – a loose and luxurious creation of velvet and silk which was feminine but

still refined. Dressing for the *thé dansant*, however, called for an altogether more elaborate garment and one that would allow for freedom of movement – a very novel idea indeed.

One of Mrs Crozier's favourite designers was Madame Lucile. Each of her delicious tango-tea frocks was given a tantalizing title – such as "You'd better ask me" and "Carnival" and were worn by the rich and famous. Fabulously luxurious fabrics like chiffon, velvet, net and fur were combined with superb artistry to create beautiful, feminine frocks.

These dresses were the creation of Messrs Boué Soeurs of the Rue de la Paix, Paris and Conduit Street, London. Glorious garments of satin draped over chiffon velours, silk and sable, black and rose shot taffetas – adorned by chenille embroidery and scalloped edges with velvet trim.

The less well-heeled could rely upon the classic little black dress with its obligatory draped skirt, whilst those who were handy with a needle and thread could make a dainty dress using one of the simple patterns featured in the well-known ladies' magazine, *Queen*. As a last resort "ordinary outdoor calling and shopping clothes" could be worn. The accoutrements that went with the London *thé dansant* outfit included an "ultra piquant" hat, possibly in black velvet adorned by an ostrich feather, black shoes and the finest of black silk stockings.

Not to be outdone, men became equally fashion-conscious and the smartest of them appeared at the *thé dansant* wearing a black morning coat, waistcoat, pin-striped trousers and black boots.

The First World War and After

THE outbreak of the First World War in 1914 put a damper on the well-established big social dances. Officers were officially forbidden to dance in uniform and even though tea dances were an excellent form of relaxation for men on a few days leave, they had to look elsewhere for their entertainment. But once the war was over tea dances rapidly reappeared on the social scene throughout the country. Besides the established clubs and hotels that opened again for business, department stores jumped on the bandwagon. In May 1919 William Whiteley's department store in Queensway, London, started holding tea dances every afternoon in their new restaurant. In Paris, theatres and music halls were converted into dancing halls, specializing in tango teas.

By 1926, there were so many tea-dance venues to choose from in London that if you were fortunate and money was no object, it was possible to tango every afternoon of the week. Costs varied tremendously depending on the venue – the Italian Roof Garden at the Criterion, with its ethereal décor, was twice as expensive as the Regent Palace Hotel. The Café de Paris and the Café Verrey in Regent Street vied for custom with Lyons Popular Café in

Before the Hammersmith Palais de Dance opened in 1919, London had never had a big dance hall. It had a good floor, a colour scheme of lights and decorative effects, continuous music and many tables for tea and talk.

Piccadilly, the Trocadero and the Georgian Restaurant at Harrods department store. Londoners seemed to have an insatiable appetite for tea-dancing and flocked to the new *palais de dance* which sprang up around the capital, offering thousands of ordinary people the chance of dancing at teatime as well as in the evenings. The Hammersmith Palais de Dance, which opened its doors in October 1919, could accommodate 2,500 people and was described as "the largest and most luxurious dancing palace in Europe". The maple wood dance floor was so valuable that dancers had to exchange their own shoes for special dance slippers. The number of boots and shoes that were left behind after the dancing was over amazed the proprietors.

> *Now that you've learnt to dance*
> *That new Brazilian prance*
> *Go on and show them all you know*
> *Dance it to and fro, Do it nice and slow.*
> *Now for your partner reach,*
> *And do the new Mattchiche*
> *It's Tango Tea-time when that*
> *melody starts.*
>
> **COME WITH ME TO THE TANGO TEA,**
> WORDS BY CON CONRAD (**STAR**, *1913*)

The Locarno Ballroom, established in 1929, boasted the only revolving bandstand in the country. Elsewhere, the tea dance became a regular feature at holiday camps, whilst those cruising on the high seas enjoyed less formal tea dances.

The popularity of "taxi boys" (professional dancing partners) increased every year in the cafés of Montparnasse, Paris. This group were waiting for partners who would pay 1 franc 50 centimes for a dance.

To Tango or Turkey Trot?

DANCE crazes came and went on the tea-dance floor: from the tango to the turkey-trot; the shimmy to the shake; the bunny hug to the black bottom and the castle walk. Another popular dance, the Lindy hop, was named after Charles Lindbergh, the American pilot who made the first solo crossing of the Atlantic in June 1927.

One of the most energetic but potentially hazardous dances was the Charleston. The first demonstration was given at a special *thé dansant* at the Carnival Club in London in 1925, to riotous results. The flapping of

legs, kicking of heels and waving of arms caused so many injuries that shortly after an extraordinary notice began to appear in the dancehalls. Patrons were implored to "Please Charleston Quietly", displayed as "P. C. Q." in many dancehalls, to try and minimize injuries.

The Second World War

IT was a sad day when, in 1936, The Savoy stopped holding *thés dansants*. But eager tango dancers were still being catered for around the corner at the Waldorf Hotel, which had been holding regular tea dances sandwiches and French fancies were replaced by frugal picnics. In peacetime, with holidays once more on the family agenda, visitors to the immensely popular Butlin's camps at Skegness and Clacton, enjoyed the regular tea dances.

Tea-dancing at the Turn of the Twenty-first Century

WHO would have thought that tea-dancing would, in a post modern era, still draw the crowds? But nostalgia and the pull of leisurely pastimes have ensured the survival, even revival, of what is essentially a most pleasurable entertainment. The early decades of the 1900s may have been the heyday of the tea dance, but now, as then, there are all sorts of venues up and down the country where you can take tea and tango. You might find yourself in a community hall in South Wales where the dance music is played on a magnificent "Christie" Wurlitzer organ, rescued from a 1930s cinema and where the tea is made by local ladies. You could even take tea dance classes at The National Theatre on the South Bank in London, or attend one of the regular tea dances held in the magnificent Floral Hall at the Royal Opera House, Covent Garden. Even though the style and sense of occasion may have changed, the dances still attract a clientele keen to tango at tea-time.

in their magnificent Palm Court restaurant since the early 1920s. The strains of Mr Mantovani's famed orchestra were heard there until the outbreak of the Second World War in September 1939.

Dancehalls and cinemas closed immediately as the blackout and threat of night raids affected evening events. But a nation at war craved amusement and informal relaxation more than ever and as the afternoon was a relatively safe time of day, tea dances continued to flourish. Huge teatime crowds clamouring for a diversion overwhelmed reopened venues. Now "swing" and "jitterbug" – imported from America – were the dances of the day. Wartime rations meant that more modest food was served and the cucumber finger

——Tearooms and Teashops——

There are many intriguing stories behind the growth in popularity of the tearoom – including the Temperance movement, the Victorian addiction to shopping and the J. Lyons Nippy waitress.

Pioneering Scots

> *There's a cozy tea room dear,*
> *Not so very far from here,*
> *Where no one else can find us,*
> *There we'll go and leave the world*
> *behind us…*

1923 SONG

By the middle of the nineteenth century Victorian society, rich and poor, had a real taste for afternoon tea. Whether it was a tea for two, a gossipy tea, a ladies-only tea or a "respite before returning home from work tea," people wanted to enjoy this new pleasure and to do so away from their homes. Glaswegians were the luckiest for they were the first to be introduced to the delights of the tearoom. It was in Glasgow in 1875 that an enterprising and adventurous young tea dealer, Mr Stuart Cranston, pioneered the idea of such an establishment. Temperance and the idea that tea was "the cup which cheers but not inebriates" certainly influenced Mr Cranston, for he had strong family connections with the movement and an eye for business and saw that working people needed somewhere to refresh themselves during the day. He was a canny Scot who noticed that leisured ladies, who had taken

to shopping as a full-time hobby, craved a place to take the weight off their tired feet during spending sprees. For, up until the appearance of the tearoom and shop, there was nowhere a Victorian lady could have a meal on her own and nowhere she could respectably meet her friends outside of the home.

Shopping was certainly important to the Victorians, but having tea was even more important, as this satirical cartoon from 1893 shows so amusingly.

Cranston's success set a new trend north of the border and by 1901 there were so many tearooms in Glasgow that the city was described as "a very Tokio for tearooms". But the most famous and distinctive venue was yet to make its debut. When Miss Cranston, Stuart's sister, opened her famous Willow Tea Rooms on fashionable Sauchiehall Street in November 1903 – she already had a small empire of

The front tearoom at The Willow showing the strange series of plaster relief panels set in a frieze. The table is set for tea.

artistic tearooms – Glaswegians were overwhelmed by its splendour. The art nouveau style was the very epitome of chic, a veritable *tour de force* of Miss Cranston's partnership with the unconventional architect, designer and artist Charles Rennie Mackintosh (1868–1928) and it set tongues wagging for months. The young architect, Edward Lutyens, was almost lost for words – and possibly a little jealous – when he described the design as "gorgeous, a wee bit vulgar…it is all quite good, all just a little *outré*", or as we would say now "over-the-top".

Refreshment in London

MEANWHILE, south of the border, there were few places that working or shopping Londoners could go for refreshment, other than the public houses where no self-respecting female would be seen. That is until 1880, when the resourceful manageress of the London Bridge branch of the Aerated Bread Company (ABC) persuaded her employers to open up a public tearoom at the back of the store. The venture proved to be as popular with ladies of high society as with shop assistants, typists and ordinary shoppers and very quickly the idea was being copied across the metropolis.

Of all the teashops to open, those belonging to J. Lyons & Co. Ltd. were undoubtedly the most popular and enduring. The very first branch opened its doors in London in 1894 at 213 Piccadilly and was an immediate success. The design was meant to stun and the French influence ensured this: the walls were lined with silk damask, the tables topped with marble and the chairs upholstered with red plush – a truly splendid place to enjoy afternoon tea and pastries. With 17 teashops to their name by 1898, the owners adopted a new "house style" and subsequent branches were resplendent with opal glass ceiling panels and walls lined in marble. Only the bentwood chairs hinted at practicality. J. Lyons & Co. Ltd. strove constantly to appeal to the widest audience and their "Popular Café", the first of which opened in London in 1904, was a testimony to this commitment. Who could fail to be attracted to a teashop which was an extravaganza of Edwardian opulence and gilt richness and which promised to provide "luxury for the millions"? Clearly not the hundreds of customers, many of them lady shoppers, who were enticed to "afternoon tea between 3 and 6" and tempted with "delicious new pastries at 2d, tea at 3d per pot and no gratuities".

Lyons continued to prosper and in 1910 a new branch was being opened approximately every two weeks. Besides London, cities including Bradford, Liverpool, Manchester and Bristol all had

The actress Binnie Hale on the cover of *Lyons Mail* in November 1930. She played the heroine in the musical comedy *Nippy*.

their Lyons teashop, as well as their Nippy waitresses. Indeed the company owed much of its success to these extraordinary ladies. In the beginning Lyons' waitresses were called "Gladys", but the name "Nippy" – very apt given the way they went about their job – was adopted following a

Nippy School

The Nippy School of Instruction was set up in 1912 by Nell Bacon, one of the very first Lyons' waitresses. She was convinced that if she had been properly trained in the 1890s, she would not have ended up emptying a cup of tea into the upturned top-hat of one of her gentlemen customers.

company competition in 1924. By then the Nippy training school had been running for 12 years, preening young women for what was considered a prestigious job. Efficient and smart, the Nippy – a great British institution in her own right – enchanted all her customers, from the royalty she served at Buckingham Palace garden parties to the humblest customer in the teashop. Wearing a black dress, starched apron, white collar, cuffs and cap, the Lyons waitress could always be relied upon to give service with a smile – and the most successful member of staff could become a "Star" Nippy and win the coveted annual prize of £100.

Tea in Paris

The Englishman abroad in Paris at the turn of the twentieth century had to look no further than the Rue de Rivoli for his cup of tea. For when the stationers, W. H. Smith, opened their first branch there in 1903, they provided customers with a tearoom where "real English tea and buns could be drunk and eaten."

A Suitable Job

A multitude of new tearooms and shops opened in London, many of them owned and managed by women, for this seemed, at the time, to be a very suitable occupation for the fairer sex. Not everyone

agreed and one expert on the subject warned, in 1902, that running a teashop was "not such a profitable business as aspiring lady teashop owners might imagine." This gloomy prospect did little to deter the pioneering women of the day, who located their establishments in the most expensive – and most prestigious – streets of London. Despite the cost of rent in fashionable Bond Street, in 1893, the Ladies' Own Tea Association opened here. This enchanting establishment was noted in the press for its dainty interior. Others soon followed suit, including The Kettledrum Tea Rooms, owned by Miss Cohen. Undaunted by any words of caution, she moved her already much-talked-about and thriving business to Old Bond Street in 1896. The charming pink and primrose décor appealed to lady shoppers and only those with strong willpower could resist the tempting delicacies produced by Messrs. Fuller, the American confectioners – renowned for their delectable iced walnut cake. The Fullers' shop, which opened in Kensington High Street in 1892, was described as "the prettiest shop in the world – all alcoves, palms and delightful décor with little tables spread for tea, which ladies will find a perfect boon".

Another venue, the Studio Tea Rooms, which started business in 1897, offered a different ambience – that of a drawing-room rather than a shop – for it was established to serve "visitors from the country and other ladies who could not afford the luxury of a club".

Fullers' Teashops

Fullers' own shops – there were 24 by 1909, including branches in Bradford and Leeds – were the height of elegance. The tea-things were white, with the word "Fullers" stamped in red on each cup and plate and each tiny pair of sugar tongs was tied up with a dainty little ribbon.

Tea and Shopping

By the mid-1880s customers in the fashionable department stores had good reason to linger, for many of these emporiums boasted their own tearooms – Whiteley's, Swan and Edgar, Derry and Toms, to name but a few. Harrods Grand Restaurant and, from 1911, their Rock Tea Gardens – situated on the roof terrace and with décor that was reminiscent of a Mediterranean garden – were amongst the recognized social rendezvous, probably the most prestigious in town. Their patrons were served tea to the melodic strains of Harrods' Royal Red Orchestra.

Further north, in Manchester, Messrs. Kendal Milne opened a tearoom in 1890, extravagantly decorated in the Moorish style, but this was not as sumptuous and mystical as Liberty's Arab Tea Room, located on the first floor of the smart Regent Street store in London. Besides serving tea in Eastern surroundings, it sold Indian condiments and, amazingly for the time, offered female visitors the ultimate convenience – a ladies' cloakroom. Sauchiehall Street in Glasgow had Pettigrew and Stephens, whose generous practice of complimentary tea for their customers ended in 1898, when a moderate charge was introduced "to remove all idea of indebtedness from the minds of patrons".

Harrods Grand Restaurant in 1909, when it featured the Royal Red Orchestra during afternoon tea.

This delightful, early 1930s tea pavilion, in the heart of Kensington Gardens, was designed by the architect J. Grey West and replaced an older decrepit building.

Popularity of Tea

As long as tea was popular the tearoom remained a firm favourite. The big names in tea like Ridgway's, Liptons and, of course, Lyons, had their venues on the high street, firmly in the public eye, but many suffered damage during the Second World War. Lyons knew that the morale boosting powers of tea were especially needed during wartime and quickly set up emergency teashops wherever there was an area of distress. A specially built Lyons commercial vehicle would tow a trailer van in camouflage, from which the public and members of the emergency services were served with free tea and buns, day and night. A truly patriotic gesture which was much appreciated by all. The last surviving Lyons teashop closed in January 1981.

Less noticeable than the high street teashop was the traditional tea pavilion,

like the one in Kensington Gardens, which was rebuilt in 1934. Today, visitors to the East Gallery of the Serpentine Gallery would never suspect that this was once a very popular tea place.

Up and down the country there are venues where the tradition of afternoon tea not only survives, but thrives. The traditional fare of delicate finger sandwiches, scones with fresh cream and jam, delicate cakes and pastries and a pot of tea is still served, whether in the grand setting of a city hotel or in a small, traditional country tearoom. Fashions come and go but the British love of tea remains undiminished for the beverage has a special place in the hearts and minds of millions of people. Given the exciting and often curious history of tea, I have no doubt that it will remain as popular for centuries to come.

where to take
Tea

Taking afternoon tea is an extremely civilized way of passing a pleasant couple of hours with friends whilst enjoying delicious food and a refreshing cup of tea. It also offers you the chance to be part of a tradition that has been popular in Britain for over 100 years.

How to Use This Guide

Choosing tea places to include has been a difficult task for there were many more which could have been mentioned. Those selected all serve an excellent traditional afternoon tea in the most congenial of surroundings and you can be sure of a warm welcome wherever you go. Some are more formal than others, but none are pretentious. I have included a range of places, from small family-run farms to exclusive hotels, museum cafés to Victorian tearooms. Many of them are in central locations, close to major tourist attractions and centres but some require just a little more effort to find.

This section is divided into two directories, the first guiding you to some of the very best places to take tea in London (see pages 47–69) and the second pointing you towards more than 25 places outside of London in England, Scotland and Wales (see pages 70–95). The entries in the London directory are listed A–Z by the name of the establishment. The second directory, "Rest of Britain" has been divided alphabetically by country, county and place name. There is also a directory listing on the opening page of each section so that you can easily find the place that you want.

Each entry starts with the full name of the establishment, where tea is taken, the address, telephone numbers, e-mail and website addresses, followed by details of opening hours and when afternoon tea is served, basic menu information, public transport or location details, advice on where to park and some ideas of other places in the area that you may like to visit. This information is followed by a description of the venue and the afternoon tea.

All of the places listed have wheelchair access and welcome children unless otherwise stated. However, it is best to telephone ahead of your visit if you have any particular requirements. Most of the places listed will cater for those with special dietary requirements but appreciate advance notice, so again it is wise to ring prior to your visit to check that your particular needs can be met.

Each place has been allocated either one, two or three teacup symbols. I want to stress that this is not an indication of quality, but a quick reference guide as to the atmosphere of the place and the kind of experience that you can expect to have when taking tea there.

🍵 Afternoon tea in a relaxed setting.
🍵🍵 A slightly more formal experience.
🍵🍵🍵 Tea in grand surroundings.

London

THE BENTLEY KEMPINSKI
27–33 Harrington Gardens
London SW7 4JX
Tel 020 7244 5555
e-mail info@thebentley-hotel.com
www.thebentley-hotel.com

Afternoon tea Daily from 3.00pm – 6.00pm (Bookings recommended)
Three set afternoon teas The Bentley Tea, Champagne Tea, Chocolate Tea & tea à la carte
Nearest underground stations Gloucester Road
Parking Valet parking (charged), meter parking
Places of interest nearby Victoria & Albert and Science and Natural History Museums, Kensington Palace and Gardens, Royal Albert Hall, Knightsbridge Shopping – Harrods & Harvey Nichols Stores, Kings Road, Brompton Cross & the boutique shops of Walton Street, High Street Kensington & Holland Park (home of summer Opera).

The Bentley is a real treasure of a find, an oasis of calm in the hurly-burly of nearby South Kensington and Gloucester Road. This grand hotel, with its acres of marble, crystal chandeliers and elegant furnishings, has been created behind the façade of three adjoining late-Victorian houses, and is sophisticated and luxurious. Comfort and service are the bywords here, and the Lobby Lounge is a most relaxing place to enjoy your afternoon tea. The elegant china

is gilt edged, the linen crisp and the food positively indulgent. Freshly prepared open sandwiches on lightly toasted bread with generous toppings are followed by bite size scones and teabreads, choux buns and the daintiest of pastries, Victoria sponge cake and macaroons. For the chocoholic, even the tiny scones are studded with pieces of chocolate. Choose your tea from a respectable list which includes The Bentley Blend and Superior Oolong, and expect the china teapot to be replaced with a fresh leaf brew regularly. A delicious experience.

THE BERKELEY
The Caramel Room
Wilton Place, Knightsbridge, London
SW1X 7RL
Tel 0207 235 6000
www.the-berkeley.co.uk

Pret-à-Portea: 2.00pm – 6.00pm every day
Wheelchair access
Nearest underground station Hyde Park Corner, Knightsbridge
Parking Limited meter and pay and display. Public car parks
Places of interest nearby Designer shops in Knightsbridge and Sloane Street including Harvey Nichols and Harrods. Hyde Park.

The Caramel Room at The Berkeley, with its chocolate coloured wall coverings, snappy faux-crocodile fabrics and cool lighting is a lovely place to relax and enjoy a very special and unusual afternoon tea after a hard day out shopping or sightseeing.

The set tea at The Berkeley is a fashionista's delight, for each delectable cake or fancy which the hotel's pastry chef produces is a miniature work of art, inspired by the latest fashions on the catwalk. Creations, which are served on fine bone china designed by Paul Smith, have included a bite sized Valentino Leopard chestnut crème handbag, an Aquascutum yellow overcoat ginger biscuit and an Yves Saint Laurent frilly passion fruit meringue! Besides all these sweet offerings you get a delectable selection of little savouries which are ideal for those watching their waistlines. Accompany this with a glass of champagne – or Couture champagne served in a Baccarat crystal glass for the ultimate fashion accessory – and a loose leaf tea chosen from a selection which includes Ceylon, Lapsang Souchon and White Peony, and you'll want to stay all afternoon. When you do leave there is a little Prêt handbag-style take-away box in pale mint green with pink handles, which is perfect to take away any unfinished delectables or as a little gift for a friend.

BROWN'S HOTEL
The English Tea Room
33–34 Albemarle Street, London W1S 4BP
Tel 020 7629 8860 ext. 6626
(recommended to book a week in advance)
e-mail
reservations.browns@roccofortehotels.com

www.roccofortehotels.com

Afternoon tea Monday to Friday 3.00pm – 6.00pm; Saturday and Sunday 2.00pm – 6.00pm
Set teas Traditional Afternoon Tea; Taittinger Champagne Afternoon Tea; Rosé Taittinger Champagne Afternoon Tea.
Wheelchair access One small step into the main entrance
Nearest underground stations Piccadilly, Green Park
Parking Public car park nearby
Places of interest nearby Royal Academy of Arts, Green Park, designer shopping on Bond Street, St James's Park

Afternoon tea has been served at Rocco Forte's Brown's ever since the hotel was created from four adjacent Georgian houses by Lord Byron's butler and his wife, Lady Byron's maid, in 1837. More than 170 years on, you would find it hard to surpass the quintessentially English surroundings

and ambience of the English Tea Room where the staff are dedicated to the highest level of service, and take care of guests with the utmost courtesy and discreet efficiency. This delightful room, with its tea tables set with the finest linen and beautiful china, is a harmonious combination of contemporary furnishings, original wood panelling and open fires. Traditional afternoon tea is served whilst a pianist tinkles on the ivories of a Baby Grand piano, and whether you have a glass of Taittinger champagne or not, your personal tiered cake stand will include a selection of finger sandwiches, fruit and plain scones served with clotted cream and strawberry jam, and the daintiest of pastries. Besides all this, and perhaps as a homage to Queen Victoria, who often took tea here, homely cakes from the trolley include a traditional Victoria sponge as well as fruit cake. Expect your sandwiches, scones and pastries to be regularly replenished, for your tea pot to be refilled with the finest loose leaf tea of your choice – including varieties from the Tregothnan English Estate in Cornwall – and for your relaxing visit to last as long as you care to linger. Situated in the heart of Mayfair, Brown's Hotel is a very popular haunt for visitors and locals alike, so be sure to book in advance.

CLARIDGE'S
The Foyer and Reading Room
Brook Street, London W1A 2JQ
Tel 020 7409 6307 (advance booking essential)

e-mail dining@claridges.co.uk
www.claridgeshoteluk.co.uk

Afternoon tea 3.00pm – 5.30pm
Three set teas Afternoon Tea, Champagne Afternoon Tea, Dom Pérignon Afternoon Tea
Seasonal set teas include Floral Champagne Afternoon Tea, Lawn Tennis Afternoon Tea, Champagne Festive Afternoon Tea
Wheelchair access
Nearest underground station Bond Street
Parking Meter parking and pay and display nearby
Places of interest nearby Wallace Collection, Bond Street and Regent Street for designer shopping
Children welcome High chairs are available (advance notice preferable)
Mobile phones Use with discretion

Art deco fans will be in seventh heaven in Claridge's, for it is a jewel of a hotel, and owes much of its splendour to the designer Basil Ionides, a 1920s pioneer of the movement. The Reading Room, with its suede walls and cut marble fireplaces is an alluring place for a very sophisticated afternoon celebration tea. Its companion room, the busier Foyer, is a remarkable blend of marble and mirrors. It features a unique silver-white light sculpture from Seattle-based artist Dale Chihuly. Comprising over 800 individually hand-blown and sculptured pieces it is hung high above a central circular leather banquette and is a definite talking point.

Claridge's is justly proud of its afternoon tea. What an experience it is to have your tea presented to you on Claridge's beautiful Bernardaud green and white porcelain by the impeccably grey-suited staff. The food, all freshly made under the direction of the maître chef des cuisines, is fit for royalty and is unusual without being pretentious. The set Afternoon Tea is designed to soothe and revive the heartiest shopper or guest; a selection of sandwiches is complemented by the most delicious and unusual apple and raisin scones, served with thick Devonshire clotted cream and its own popular tea-infused Marco-Polo jelly. Make sure you leave some room for the exquisite French pastries that follow: the selection changes daily and might include chocolate roulade, strawberry tartlets or vanilla millefeuille. Claridge's also helps caters to events in the social calendar – for example, when the Chelsea Flower Show is blooming there is the special Floral Champagne menu. There are special Thanksgiving and Easter teas, and

what could be more traditional than succulent strawberries and cream with your Lawn Tennis Afternoon Tea during the tennis season? The choices don't end here for Claridge's offers more than 30 different varieties of tea, many of which have been carefully selected for them by Mariage Frères, the oldest French importer of tea. Amongst the selection are favourites such as the traditional Claridge's Royal blend, but for the more adventurous there is the fabulous Royal White-Silver Needles – picked on only two days of the year at dawn and processed entirely by hand – as well as three teas from the small exclusive crops grown, nurtured and hand picked by the Tregothnan English Estate in Cornwall. If you thought this was the end, then think again, for there are a number of excellent champagnes to complement your tea – Laurent Perrier Brut NV or Grand Siècle and Dom Pérignon 1996 or 1998.

Whenever you visit Claridge's for tea there will be a pianist and violinist playing soothing music, so sit back, relax and revel in the ultimate tea experience.

THE DORCHESTER
The Promenade
Park Lane, London W1K 1QA
Tel 020 7629 8888 ext 691 (for tea reservations)
e-mail restaurant@thedorchester.com
www.thedorchester.com

Afternoon tea 2.30pm – 6.30pm; two sittings: 2.30pm or 4.45pm
Three set afternoon teas The Dorchester Champagne Afternoon Tea, The Dorchester Afternoon Tea, High Tea; tea à la carte also available (minimum charge made)
Wheelchair access
Nearest underground station Hyde Park Corner
Parking None, except by prior arrangement with the hotel; public car park nearby
Places of interest nearby Apsley House, Buckingham Palace, Albert Memorial, Victoria and Albert Museum, Museum of Mankind, shopping in Knightsbridge and Bond Street

Taking tea in The Promenade, the focal point of The Dorchester since it opened in 1931, has to be one of the most enjoyable and special tea experiences imaginable. From the moment you cross the threshold of this wonderful space, with its luxurious and elegant décor, magnificent floral arrangements and intimate table seating, you can be certain of experiencing an afternoon of sheer indulgence. The ambience is relaxed, the service impeccable, and no detail has been overlooked, from the soft strains of the resident pianist, to the beautiful silver-edged bone china and crisp linen tablecloths, to the silverware and fresh flowers on each table.

The Dorchester's award-winning afternoon tea, which combines tradition with innovation, is simply quite delectable. A changing selection of finger sandwiches on a variety of home-baked breads are the prelude to a surprise pre-dessert treat, followed by melt-in-the-mouth scones served with both strawberry and a seasonal jam – and, of course, clotted cream. The crowning glory to this mini-feast, in pride of place on the top tier of the silver cake stand is a choice of delectable French pastries created by the patissier. Add a glass of champagne to this and you have a truly celebratory tea. Whilst the most popular tea is "The Dorchester House Blend" a selection

of more than 20 leaf teas is available and as you would expect from a venue of this calibre, many of these are rare varieties.

Tea in The Promenade at The Dorchester is a truly memorable experience. The hotel will even arrange birthday cakes and flowers if you are celebrating a special occasion. It is hardly surprising that guests are as reluctant to leave as they are eager to arrive.

FORTNUM & MASON
St James's Restaurant
181 Piccadilly, London W1A 1ER
Tel 020 7734 8040
e-mail info@fortnumandmason.com
www.fortnumandmason.com

Afternoon tea 3.00pm – 6.00pm daily (store opening hours differ). Advance reservation recommended.

Two set teas Traditional Champagne Afternoon Tea, Champagne High Tea

Nearest underground stations Green Park, Piccadilly

Places of interest nearby Buckingham Palace, Royal Academy of Arts, Bond Street, Burlington Arcade

Crossing the threshold into Fortnum & Mason – famed for its chiming clock – is like stepping into an Aladdin's cave, for the ground floor is filled with the most sublime displays of extraordinarily luxurious food. This should give you an inkling of the treat that awaits you at teatime.

A number of restaurants within the store serve afternoon tea, but the most elegant is, without doubt, the St James's Restaurant on the fourth floor. The tables are laid with linen and fine china and three set tea menus are on offer. For the greediest (or hungriest) guest there is the High Tea – a positive feast of Fortnum's famous Welsh Rarebit or Scrambling Highlander (scrambled eggs and smoked salmon on granary toast) followed by plain and fruit scones, Somerset clotted cream and Fortnum's strawberry preserve and a choice of pastries from the Classic selection. If you choose the Traditional tea, you will be able to feast on a miniature open sandwich of London Smoked Salmon with Crème Fraiche and lime, an array of finger sandwiches with delicious fillings as well as the scones and pastries. Add a glass of Brut Reserve or Rosé champagne to either of these set teas and make this a real celebration. As for the tea itself, which was Fortnum's first speciality and remains close to the hearts of its customers three centuries later, the choice is exceptional and unsurpassable. Tea guests may choose from the Classic Selection, which has favourites such as Royal or Queen Anne Blend as well as Lapsang Souchon and Ceylon Orange Pekoe, or from the Rare Selection, which offers the aristocratic Assam Hazelbank, Second Flush Darjeeling Bannockburn and Darjeeling Singbulli Oolong.

FOUR SEASONS HOTEL
The Lounge
Hamilton Place, London W1A 1AZ
Tel 020 7499 0888 ext. 5334 (for tea reservations)
e-mail fsh.london@fourseasons.com
www.fourseasons.com/london/dining/the _lounge.html

Afternoon tea 3.00pm – 7.00pm
Two set afternoon teas Traditional Afternoon Tea, Champagne Afternoon Tea; tea à la carte also available
Nearest underground stations Hyde Park, Piccadilly
Parking Hotel car park (payable)
Places of interest nearby Hyde Park, Knightsbridge, Apsley House

Many guests still refer to the Four Seasons Hotel by its original name, The Inn on the Park – a testimony to the loyalty they feel towards this modern but immensely traditional hotel. Renowned for the attention to personal service, the ambience in The Lounge is one of relaxed comfort, with sofas and settees set in conversational groups for intimacy.

Apart from the Traditional Afternoon Tea, the Four Seasons is renowned for its Champagne Afternoon Tea, which is designed to tantalise the taste buds. Every season the executive chef creates an adventurous themed tea menu which not only reflects the time of year, but takes advantage of the best produce available. So, Spring tea might start with a savoury crêpe, a selection of sandwiches with deliciously unusual fillings, as diverse as new season mushroom and sorrel cream cheese or marinated salmon trout, followed by scones, clotted cream and strawberry-rhubarb jam. The sweets that follow are divine – there could be layered coconut-carrot cake with raspberries, and rhubarb and Pimm's meringue. Not to be overlooked is the splendid range of loose teas which includes Queen Mary (a Darjeeling blend that was the personal choice of the late Queen Mary) and Twinings specially created (Silver) Anniversary Blend. Taking tea at this hotel is a real treat for a special celebration.

HARRODS
The Georgian Restaurant
Brompton Road, London SW1X 7XL
Tel 020 7225 6800 (for tea bookings)
e-mail catering@harrods.com
www.Harrods.com

Afternoon Tea Monday to Saturday 3.45pm – 7.00pm; Sunday 12.00pm – 6.00pm (store opening hours differ)
Two set teas Best Afternoon Tea in London, Champagne Afternoon Tea
Nearest underground station Knightsbridge
Parking Store car park (payable)
Places of interest nearby Sloane Street for designer boutiques, Victoria and Albert Museum, Natural History Museum, Science Museum, Royal Albert Hall, Hyde Park

Of the 20 restaurants within Harrods, Britain's largest department store, the Georgian Restaurant is undoubtedly the flagship. The décor is every bit as grand as when Victor Silvester, the great band leader, had tea here in the 1930s and the resident pianist, who plays every day, adds to your enjoyment.

Full afternoon tea arrives very grandly on a silver stand and is a lovely selection of mini sandwiches, Harrods scones with clotted cream and preserves and dainty tea pastries. The menu choice of Harrods tea includes their own Afternoon Blend and the ever popular Darjeeling, Lapsang Souchong and Assam, but you are invited to ask for any other unlisted variety that you especially like. For tea connoisseurs this could be heaven, as the store, which originally opened as a tea merchant and grocery store in 1849, sells an enviable range of thirst-quenching premium blends in the magnificent Food Hall, over 160 varieties. One exclusive is Hand-Twisted Organic Darjeeling, but as this is only available in very limited quantities, it is unlikely to ever feature on the afternoon tea menu. Console yourself instead with a purchase from the caddy collection – second flush Darjeeling Margaret's Hope or Castleton perhaps.

Harrods operate a strict dress code – no ripped jeans or scruffy clothing – and mobile phones are banned throughout the store. Harrods is a hive of activity, and

The Georgian Restaurant may not be as quiet as some would like. However, you can be sure of the most courteous and warm attention from the waiting staff, whose aim is to make your visit a memorable and enjoyable occasion.

KENSINGTON PALACE
The Orangery
The State Apartments, Kensington Palace, Kensington Gardens, London W8 3UY
Tel 020 7938 1406
e-mail orangery@digbytrout.co.uk
www.digbytrout.co.uk/branches/ kensington

Afternoon tea 1 November to 28 February 10.00am – 5.00pm; 1 March to 21 October 10.00am – 6.00pm
Set afternoon teas English Tea, Orangery Tea, Champagne Tea, Tregothnan English Tea; tea à la carte also available
Wheelchair access
Nearest underground stations Queensway, Gloucester Road, High Street Kensington
Parking Public car park on Bayswater Road
Places of interest nearby Kensington Palace, Serpentine Gallery, Princess Diana Memorial Playground, Kensington Gardens

The magnificent eighteenth-century Orangery, situated within the grounds of Kensington Palace where Queen Victoria

was born, is a busy and bustling place for tea, but one which still manages to retain its sense of history and grandeur. Sitting here, amidst the tranquil haven of Kensington Gardens, you can almost imagine Queen Anne and her aristocratic guests dining here in the summer months.

A heavily laden table of delectable home-made scones, shortbreads, fruit slices and wholesome cakes greets you as you walk in the door and you'll find it quite a challenge deciding what to eat. You could always settle for one of the set teas rather than ordering à la carte. Besides the Light Tea, the Orangery Tea and the Champagne Tea, there is the superlative Tregothnan English Tea, resplendent with tea sandwiches, mini scones with clotted cream and jam, afternoon tea cakes and dainty pastries, champagne, and to complete the event, a choice of teas from the Cornish Tregothnan Estate. These, and a good selection of other bagged and loose leaf teas, are also on offer à la carte. The staff here are friendly and helpful, and this, as well as the close proximity of the Princess Diana Memorial Playground, helps to make the Orangery a very popular destination for families.

The only slight drawbacks of the Orangery are that at busy times you may have to queue outside and also the toilets are situated in a separate small building a short walk away. These things aside, you can expect to pass a very pleasant couple of hours, and you could always visit the palace afterwards.

KENWOOD HOUSE
The Brew House, Hampstead Lane, London NW3 3JR
Tel 020 8341 5384
e-mail info@companyofcooks.com
www.companyofcooks.com

Afternoon tea March to September 9.00am – 6.00pm; October 9.00am – dusk; November to February 9.00am – 4.00pm; Boxing Day and New Year's Day 10.00am – 3.30pm. Closed Christmas Eve and Christmas Day.
Tea à la carte only
Nearest underground stations Hampstead Heath, Highgate
Parking At Kenwood House
Places of interest nearby Hampstead Heath, Keats House

I'm an enthusiastic walker and the Brew House, set in the service wing of Kenwood House, is a wonderful place for a rest and refreshment after a long trek across Hampstead Heath. It is also very popular with locals and visitors to the house itself, an imposing eighteenth-century villa which houses the Iveagh Bequest, an internationally renowned collection of paintings you should try to visit if you have time. Take a look at the walls in the Brew House while you are deciding what to eat, for they have been cleverly decorated to resemble a Print Room, but all the vistas and views are trompe l'oeil.

This self-service restaurant offers deliciously wholesome, home-made food, but there is no set tea menu. At any time of the day you can expect to find baskets piled high with jumbo scones, served with whipped cream and preserves and cakes such as chocolate fudge, carrot and sticky toffee date. Cream cakes and Danish pastries add to the temptation, so resist if you can! Bagged tea comes from a long-established supplier in nearby Muswell Hill and besides the old favourites – Assam and Earl Grey – you can select Gunpowder green tea and organic Ceylon.

On a dry, bright day the outside terrace with its landscaped garden is a delightful place to sit, gossip and sip your tea. Just be sure to wrap up warm in the winter!

café-restaurant. Many of the original fittings, including the vast brick ovens with their ornate cast iron doors and Royal Coat of Arms, have been lovingly preserved, and these add greatly to the ambience of the place. The atmosphere is far from formal and you get what the owners describe as "proper food and cake", all home-baked. You have to order at the counter but your food – perhaps including their award-winning scones or speciality Lemon Florentine – is then brought to the table. Both leaf and bagged tea are served; the range includes the usual favourites as well as some 20 or more herbal teas and infusions. In the summer, striped awnings and umbrellas on the piazza shade you

---

THE KEW GREENHOUSE CAFÉ
1 Station Parade, Kew Gardens, Surrey TW9 3PS
Tel 020 8940 0183
www.thekewgreenhouse.co.uk

Opening hours 8.00am – dusk
Tea à la carte
Nearest underground station Kew Gardens
Parking Meter parking
Places of interest nearby Royal Botanic Gardens, National Archives
The Kew Greenhouse, resplendent with its abundance of foliage and greenery, was built in 1895 and served as the village bakery for many years before eventually evolving into a fully-fledged tearoom and

from the sun. Not the place for a celebration tea, but somewhere you can be sure you will get wholesome, fresh food and a refreshing pot of tea.

THE LANDMARK LONDON
Winter Garden
222 Marylebone Road, London NW1 6JQ
Tel 020 7631 8000 (no bookings taken)
Fax 020 7631 8080
e-mail dining@thelandmark.co.uk
www.landmarklondon.co.uk

Afternoon tea 3.00pm – 6.00pm
Two set teas The Winter Garden Tea and The Landmark Tea; tea à la carte also available, with a minimum charge for non-residents – please check when ordering
Nearest underground station Marylebone
Parking Underground parking for 80 cars, meters and pay and display nearby
Places of interest nearby Madame Tussauds, The Planetarium

Walking into the Winter Garden at the Landmark London, with its soaring glass-roofed eight-storey atrium, palm trees and amazing feeling of light and space, is a breathtaking experience. Originally opened in 1899 as one of the great Victorian railway termini hotels – the Winter Garden was the vast central courtyard – it still retains the character, elegance and grandeur of a bygone era. Despite its popularity and informality, there is an aura of comfortable, calm perfection about the place (mobile

phones are discouraged), an ambience which is reflected in the beautifully served, award-winning afternoon tea.

The tea here is a positive feast and everything is freshly prepared on the day, in the hotel's own pastry department. Assorted sandwiches and dainty Viennese bridge rolls, as well as plain and fruit scones with clotted cream and strawberry jam, compete with elegant French pastries for room on your plate. The Landmark Tea, one of the two set teas on offer, includes strawberries and cream and champagne and is tailor-made for that

extra special occasion. With a good selection of loose teas, including Tregothnan from Cornwall, Lapsang Souchong, Green Gunpowder, Russian Caravan, Darjeeling, Assam and Earl Grey Blue Flower as well as tisanes, exotic black

Afternoon tea Monday to Saturday
3.30pm – 6.00pm; Sunday 4.00pm –
6.00pm
Two set teas The Lanesborough Tea or
The Belgravia Tea. Tea à la carte (set
minimum charge applies)
Nearest underground station Hyde Park
Corner
Parking Hotel valet parking
Places of interest nearby Hyde Park,
Knightsbridge, Admiralty Arch, Apsley
House

There is the most wonderful feeling of light
and space as you walk into The
Lanesborough's beautiful glass-roofed
Conservatory, and fortunately the tea
experience that awaits you is equal to the
delightful surroundings. The tables are set
with crisp linen and bone china, gentle
piano music creates a relaxing atmosphere,
teas and fruit infusions, there is a tea to
and the staff are attentive and courteous.
suit every taste. The gentle and relaxing
Both of the set teas include the most
strains of a grand piano, accompanied by a
delicious finger sandwiches and bite-sized
violin, harp or flute, add to the pleasure of
quiches, scones and miniature toasted tea
tea in the Winter Garden, which is a truly
cakes, as well as individual tea breads and
delightful experience.
delectable pastries. Try some of the
wonderful home-made lemon curd on
your scone for a real burst of flavour. For

THE LANESBOROUGH
even more of a treat, have the Belgravia
The Conservatory
Tea, which starts off with strawberries and
1 Lanesborough Place, Hyde Park Corner,
cream, as well as your choice of a glass of
London SW1X 7TA
bubbly or a Kir Royal. Whether you choose
Tel 020 7259 5599
the Lanesborough Tea – delicious home-
(ask for the Conservatory)
made traditional fare plus crumpets and
e-mail info@lanesborough.com
English tea-breads, the Belgravia Tea –
www.lanesborough.co.uk
the Lanesborough with the addition of

strawberries, cream and a glass of

to a glorious afternoon tea in an unusual but very comfortable setting, the Conservatory is to be recommended.

LOUIS PATISSERIE
32 Heath Street, Hampstead, London NW3 6TE
Tel 020 7435 9908

Opening hours 9.00am – 6.00pm
Tea à la carte
Nearest underground station Hampstead
Parking Pay and display nearby
Places of interest nearby Historic Hampstead Village, Hampstead Heath, Keats House, Fenton House

champagne, an afternoon champagne cocktail or tea à la carte, you'll be served with courtesy. Drinking tea here is exceptionally worthwhile, for the Lanesborough prides itself on a daily tasting of their teas by their "tea sommelier" to ensure quality and consistency of flavour. The list includes some unusual varieties of leaf such as Assam Golden Tippy Mokalbari, Hajua Estate White Assam and Pu-erh (aged) as well as their unique and exclusive Afternoon Blend, consisting of Darjeeling, China Keemum and whole rose buds. Only leaf tea is served here, but there is not a tea strainer in sight. The secret lies in the strainer ingeniously fitted inside the teapot.

So, whether you are exhausted from a day's shopping in nearby Knightsbridge or just want to relax, unwind or treat yourself

Louis Patisserie is a real institution in Hampstead and the shop's distinctive pink cartons and bags can be seen all around the area. The tiny tea lounge, which was founded in 1963 by Louis Permayer, retains a charming old-fashioned, continental feel and is regularly patronized by the local literati, thespians and singers. Louis's personal influence is very evident for he continues to work in the bakery attached to the tea lounge. You can eat here at any time of the day, but for your teatime treat choose from the extensive daily selection of croissants, Danish pastries, fruit tarts, meringues, scones and cream cakes. All of these, and more, are temptingly displayed in the window and everything is freshly baked on the premises. Four different types of tea, both leaf and bagged, are available and are served in china cups and saucers. This is a welcoming and informal place to relax and rest when shopping or sightseeing. You can always buy a little something to take home with you as well.

THE MONTAGUE ON THE GARDENS
The Conservatory
15 Montague Square, Bloomsbury, London WC1B 5BJ
Tel 020 7612 8414 (for tea reservations)
Fax 020 7637 2516
e-mail bookmt@rchmail.com
www.montaguehotel.com

Afternoon tea 3.00pm – 6.00pm
Two set teas Cream Tea, High Tea; tea à la carte also available
Nearest underground stations Russell Square, Holborn
Parking Limited meter parking in area
Places of interest nearby British Museum, Covent Garden

The time-honoured tradition of afternoon tea is celebrated every afternoon in the delightful sunlit conservatory of the Montague on the Gardens. Overlooking a peaceful and secluded garden square and adjacent to the world famous British Museum, the conservatory is also ideally situated for visitors to literary Bloomsbury and Covent Garden. Comfort and luxury are combined in these charming surroundings, and the tea is a positive pleasure. Silverware, china and flowers adorn the tables and only the finest leaf tea is served, although the range of 10 teas available is fairly standard. As well as tea à la carte there are two set teas to choose between. The traditional Cream Tea consists of freshly-baked scones, jam and that most slimming of toppings, delicious Devonshire clotted cream. The High Tea, has, in addition to all this, finger sandwiches and pastries of the day. Very comforting food indeed. In the summer the garden terrace here really is a delightful place to take tea.

NATIONAL PORTRAIT GALLERY
The Portrait Restaurant
St Martin's Place, London WC2 0HE
Tel 020 7312 2490
e-mail portrait.restaurant@searcys.co.uk
www.npg.org.uk

Afternoon tea 3.00pm – 5.00pm
Two set teas Portrait Tea, Champagne Tea; tea à la carte also available

Nearest underground stations Leicester Square, Charing Cross
No parking
Places of interest nearby Covent Garden, National Gallery, Trafalgar Square

The vista from this restaurant, where a very good traditional afternoon tea is served every day, is not so much a "portrait" as a "landscape", and a spectacular one at that. No matter where you sit in this stylish modern room, you get a panoramic view of Nelson's Column, Big Ben and the Houses of Parliament, which makes it one of London's wonderful hidden treasures.

You don't have to have a set tea here to enjoy the large fluffy scones, golden clotted cream and preserves, or the homemade cakes and biscuits – including lavender shortbread. If you choose the Portrait Tea you will also get a selection of delicious house sandwiches as well as a slice of homemade cake. On the other hand you could opt for the more glamorous Champagne Tea, with its open smoked salmon sandwich, cake, scones with all the trimmings, plus a glass of bubbly. Only bagged tea is served here and you'll have to ask for hot water. The staff are young, the service artistically indifferent and if you sit near the bar and service area, it can be a bit noisy. Still, the atmosphere is very relaxed, the tea is good and it's a super place to rest after a visit to the stunning Portrait Gallery rooms downstairs. Even on a dull wet day a visit here is an energizing experience.

THE ORIGINAL MAIDS OF HONOUR
288 Kew Road, Richmond, Surrey
TW9 3DU
Tel 020 8940 2752
www.theoriginalmaidsofhonour.co.uk

Afternoon tea Tuesday to Saturday 2.30pm – 5.30pm. Closed bank holidays.
One set tea or tea à la carte
Nearest underground station Kew Gardens
Parking On-street parking
Places of interest nearby Royal Botanic Gardens, National Archives

For many visitors, The Original Maids of Honour is exactly what a teashop should be – quaint, quirky and quintessentially English. The old world, nostalgic feel is everywhere, from the bow-fronted windows, chintz curtains, open log fire, oak tables and wheelback chairs to the crocheted lace doilies, willow pattern china and collection of teapots. There's also a small terrace with tables outside where you can sip your tea on a nice summer day.

The Maids of Honour cake, after which the shop is named, is a real curiosity and definitely worth a try. Legend has it that

King Henry VIII ate these cakes whilst he was at Richmond Palace and liked them so much that he ordered that the recipe be locked in an iron box and kept secret. Its recipe remains a Newens' family secret to this day. Like everything else here, you can tell that the fluffy scones are home-made because they are delightfully different shapes. On busy days you may be asked to share a table and you can then compare notes with your fellow tea connoisseurs about the lovely cakes and pastries.

PETER DE WIT'S CAFÉ
21 Greenwich Church Street, London SE10 9BJ
Tel/Fax 020 8305 0048
e-mail janedewit@yahoo.co.uk
www.peterdewitscafe.com

Opening hours Monday to Friday 10.00am – 6.00pm; Saturday, Sunday and bank holidays 9.30am – 6.00pm
Cream tea and tea à la carte
Nearest underground station North Greenwich
Parking Public car parks nearby
Places of interest nearby Cutty Sark, National Maritime Museum, Greenwich Old Royal Observatory, Fan Museum, Rangers House

A treasure in the midst of historic Greenwich and very popular with tourists, the de Wit's tiny café is situated within the oldest house in the district. Dating back, in part, to the fifteenth century, the interior is plain and simple but you can be sure of a warm welcome and excellent service from the young, enthusiastic staff. The emphasis is on quality and only the finest, often organic, ingredients are used in the preparation of their food. Scones are served with unsalted French butter, double or clotted cream and preserves, the huge sandwiches have classic fillings and the home-baked cakes are served in pudding size portions. Expect to find Carrot Cake and Apple Crumble Cake, both favourites, as well as a light and a rich fruit cake.

There are five Indian and two China teas to choose from as well as a range of herbal and fruit infusions. Even though tables are in demand at the weekends, you won't find yours being cleared as soon as you finish the last crumb of cake. Weekdays are certainly more leisurely and you can linger as long as you like, do the crossword or play chess whilst you enjoy the interesting background music. There are so many tourist attractions in the vicinity that you could have a light lunch here and then return for a scrumptious tea later in the day.

THE RITZ
The Palm Court
150 Piccadilly, London W1J 9BR
Tel 020 7493 8181 (reservations essential, at least four weeks in advance)
Fax 020 7493 2687
e-mail enquire@theritzlondon.com
www.theritzlondon.com (for on-line tea bookings)

Afternoon tea Five sittings: 11.30am, 1.30pm, 3.30pm, 5.30pm, 7.30pm
One set tea
Wheelchair access A few steps up to the Palm Court
Nearest underground stations Green Park, Piccadilly
Parking Valet parking
Places of interest nearby Royal Academy of Arts, Green Park, Saville Row, Burlington Arcade, Bond Street

Formal dress code No jeans or trainers. Gentlemen must wear a jacket and tie
Mobile phones discouraged

The world famous Palm Court in Cesar Ritz's gracious Edwardian hotel, located in the heart of St James's, is the epitome of sophistication and elegance and the afternoon tea the height of decadence and luxury. You know that you are about to enjoy a very special experience as you take the few steps up to the Palm Court from the ground floor's central gallery area, passing between a pair of grand Ionic

marbled columns. Pretty Louis XVI chairs, marble-topped tables beautifully set with crisp linen and delicate china await the guests eager to share in what is a quintessentially Ritz experience.

If you are an aspiring tea guest, you must book your table several weeks in advance. I can promise you that the wait will be well worth it, for the afternoon tea is quite superb, the service very attentive and although you will be limited to how long you can stay by the next sitting, there is no real sense of pressure on you to "eat up". Alongside the selection of dainty sandwiches made on different breads are freshly-baked apple and raisin scones, clotted cream and organic strawberry preserve, afternoon tea pastries and fruits-of-the-forest compote with English cream. It's impossible to leave feeling hungry, as the Ritz feast is regularly replenished by the staff. A choice from thirteen varieties of leaf tea completes the occasion, for an "occasion" is exactly what tea in the Palm Court is. When you start to suffer from "Ritz" withdrawal symptoms, you'll find the recipe for their wonderful Marble Cake and other delectable items in *The London Ritz Book of Afternoon Tea.*

THE RUBENS AT THE PALACE
The Palace Lounge
39 Buckingham Palace Road, London SW1W 0PS
Tel 020 7834 6600 (booking recommended)
Fax 020 7828 5401
e-mail bookrb@rchmail.com
www.rubenshotel.com

Afternoon tea 2.30pm – 5.00pm
Set teas Traditional Afternoon Tea, Royal Palace High Tea, Original Crumpet Tea, Devonshire Cream Tea, Gingerbread men; tea à la carte also available
Nearest underground station Victoria
Parking Public car park near Victoria coach station

Places of interest nearby Buckingham Palace, Green Park, St James's Park
Just a stone's throw from Buckingham Palace, close by beautiful St James's Park, Green Park, The Mall and with a view of Buckingham Palace Royal Mews, the Palace Lounge at The Rubens is a very enticing haven for a highly-rated traditional afternoon tea. Comfortable wing chairs and sofas add to the relaxed but refined atmosphere and the service is

efficient and attentive but discreet. This probably explains why the lounge was so popular in the 1940s with General Sikorski, Commander-in-Chief of the Free Polish Forces, who took tea here every day, accompanied on one occasion by General de Gaulle.

Afternoon tea at The Rubens is fit for royalty – and presented royally on an elegant tiered silver stand. From the Devonshire Cream Tea of scones, the traditional trimmings and a choice of tea, you can move up a notch to the Traditional Afternoon Tea with the addition of finger sandwiches, tea pastries and fruitcake. Replace the scones with freshly baked crumpets and you have the

Original Crumpet Tea. Higher still up the scale is the Royal Palace High Tea, which has all the elements of the Traditional Tea, with the addition of a glass of champagne. Your tea itself – you can request either leaf or bagged and choose from 10 different varieties – is served in a silver teapot and accompanied by the all important jug of hot water. If you are visiting in the summer, why not visit Buckingham Palace first, then after your delicious tea take a stroll to Westminster, Harrods or the London Eye.

THE SAVOY
Thames Foyer
Strand, London WC2R 0EU
Tel 020 7420 2669 (booking advisable for afternoon tea)
Fax 020 7240 6040
e-mail savoy.dining@fairmont.com
www.fairmont.com/savoy

Afternoon tea Monday to Friday 2.00pm – 5.30pm; Saturday and Sunday 12.00noon – 5.00pm
Set teas Traditional Afternoon Tea, The Savoy Champagne Afternoon Tea
The Savoy English Theatre Tea is also served, between 5.30pm – 7.30pm.
Wheelchair access Portable ramp available for stairs down to the Foyer
Nearest underground stations Charing Cross, Covent Garden, Embankment
Parking Adelphi Garage nearby
Places of interest nearby Somerset

House, Festival Hall, National Theatre, Savoy Theatre, Covent Garden, Royal Opera House
Dress code Smart jeans are allowed, but no trainers

SAVOY
LONDON

As you descend the elegant staircase to the Thames Foyer of the Savoy you can't help but notice an aura of restrained elegance and grandeur, evocative of times past. The décor is wonderful, from the trompe l'oeil mural of a romantic garden to the three spectacular art deco mirrors which adorn another wall. It was in these marvellous surroundings that Rudolph Valentino danced and where George Gershwin played *Rhapsody In Blue*. The tranquil ambience is complemented by the discreet but totally attentive service and guests may linger in the deep sofas and armchairs for as long as they like, whilst listening to the delicate strains of the piano. The set tea of delicate finger sandwiches, delectable bite-size French pastries, plain and fruit scones – all made in the hotel's patisserie – served with clotted cream and strawberry preserve, arrives on a three-tiered silver stand, served by waiters in tail coats. Don't worry if you can't finish all the cakes – a "doggy" bag can easily be arranged! The Savoy English Theatre Tea is wonderful innovation, for it combines all the delights of a traditional afternoon tea with some more substantial food, just like High Tea, and makes an excellent pre-theatre treat.

Connoisseurs of tea will be spoilt for choice as the Savoy offers a distinctive collection of leaf teas. Besides their own Special Blend of tea – a robust black tea blended from Indian, Kenyan and Sri Lankan leaves, there are three Savoy Favourites – Tiger Hill, a Nilgiri Hills tea, Lapsang Souchon Butterfly and Fairmont Earl Grey. Add to these a choice of Green teas, Green Flavoured Teas, Oolong, Darjeeling – Margaret's Hope and Castelton, a premium second flush tea – Assam and Ceylon teas, as well as Black Flavoured Teas, decaffeinated teas, White Tea and a selection of Herbal and Fruit Infusions, you realize that tea is taken very seriously here. And before you leave you can purchase any of the Savoy teas in specially designed caddies, or if you feel in need of a souvenir, why not buy a copy of Anton Edelman's book, *Taking Tea at the Savoy*, before you leave?

TEA PALACE
175 Westbourne Grove, London W11 2SB
Tel 020 7727 2600
Fax 020 7727 0006
e-mail info@teapalace.co.uk
www.teapalace.co.uk

Opening hours 10.00am – 7.00pm for all sorts of food
Afternoon Tea Daily 3.00pm – 7.00pm

Open bank holidays, except during Notting Hill Carnival
Two set teas Palace Tea, Champagne Tea; also an à la carte tea menu and regular Tea Tastings
Nearest underground stations Notting Hill and Bayswater Underground stations
Places of interest nearby Portobello Road Market, Notting Hill designer shops, Kensington Gardens

Tea at the chic Tea Palace is something special and not to be missed. From the moment you cross the threshold of this stylish emporium, you know that tea is taken very seriously, for there are dozens of tea caddies lining the wall behind the counter, all in the signature colours of purple and amethyst embellished with a crown. Neither grand hotel nor nostalgic teashop, Tea Palace is a divine place to enjoy a traditional afternoon tea in very comfortable surroundings. The tea room is light and airy, the table linen crisp and white, the white bone china with its distinctive purple crown is impeccable, and the staff are knowledgeable, helpful and attentive. The selection of tea on offer is astonishing, with over 150 leaf teas sourced from around the world, exceeding any other tea emporium in London. There may be a little less choice as far as food goes, but you would have to go a long way to beat the light fluffy scones served with organic clotted cream and jam, the dainty cakes and the finger sandwiches which make up the Palace Tea. If you prefer, there are also toasted crumpets, shortbread biscuits and wholesome carrot and honey cake on offer. Once your appetite is satisfied, you can browse amongst the tea caddies and vast array of tea-related gifts on sale in the shop, and maybe take home a memento of a special afternoon tea.

THE WALLACE RESTAURANT
The Wallace Collection, Hertford House, Manchester Square, London W1U 3BN
Tel 020 7563 9505
e-mail reservations@thewallacerestaurant.com
www.wallacecollection.org

Afternoon Tea Daily 3.00pm – 5.00pm. Closed bank holidays
Two set teas The Parisien and The Wallace; tea à la carte also available
Nearest underground stations Bond Street, Baker Street
Plces of interest nearby Wallace Collection, Bond Street and Oxford Street shops

What more stunning venue could there be for tea in Central London than The

Wallace, the restaurant situated in the beautiful Sculpture Garden of Hertford House, home to the Wallace Art Collection? As you make your way to the informal but elegant restaurant, you can't help but notice the wonderful paintings by artists such as Titian, Rembrandt, Hals (The Laughing Cavalier) and Velázquez. Seated at tables amongst beautiful trees beneath the fabulous glass atrium roof, this is a positively charming place to while away an hour or so. The set afternoon teas have a distinctive Parisian feel about them, and are far from traditional. Here, the finger sandwiches and fine French pastries are accompanied by either a classic "Croque Monsieur" (and ask for it without ham if you prefer) or, for a deluxe experience, homemade foie gras and brioche. Add your choice of tea from the list of more than 20 loose leaf on offer – including favourites like Darjeeling and Assam and the more unusual China White Silver needles – and maybe a glass of champagne, and you are all set for a last look at the exquisite art collection before you leave.

Rest of Britain

AVON
SEARCY'S AT THE PUMP ROOM
9 Stall Street, Bath BA1 1LZ
Tel 01225 444477
Fax 01225 447979
e-mail pumproom@milburn.co.uk
www.searcys.co.uk

Opening hours From 9.30am.
Afternoon tea From 2.30pm to close;
closing times vary according to the time of
year. Bookings taken for weekdays only; a
queuing system operates at weekends.
Two set teas Traditional Pump Room Tea,
Searcy's Champagne Tea
Wheelchair access Fully accessible. Level
access from Abbey Church Yard
Location Opposite Bath Abbey, within the
Roman Baths building
Parking Several public car parks nearby
Places of interest nearby The Abbey,
Roman Baths, Pump Room, Costume
Museum, Royal Crescent

The Pump Room has been Bath's favourite
meeting place since it was built by Thomas
Baldwin and John Palmer in 1795. Then it
was the focal point of fashionable society
who congregated there to socialize and
"take the waters". The elegance and
classical Georgian charm of the room has
hardly changed since it was built and it's no
wonder that Jane Austen sent the heroine
of her novel Persuasion here in the hope of
bumping into her beau. Whilst the
fictional Catherine and Mr Tilney may
have sampled the spa water, which still
flows from the fountain overlooking the
natural hot spring, it's doubtful that they
would have enjoyed the delicious afternoon
teas that are served here now.

Seated at tables set with crisp linen under
a wonderful glass chandelier, you can choose
from a set afternoon tea with tea
sandwiches, scones, clotted cream and
preserves as well as Pump Room cakes and
pastries, or go for the Champagne Tea with
its smoked salmon and cucumber
sandwiches in addition to the scones, cakes
and pastries. For the fainthearted there is
always the traditional Bath Bun served here
with cinnamon butter, or a choice of cakes
from the Tea Time Bakery – the spicy
orange and cranberry cake has a sticky
marmalade glaze which is hard to resist, and
the coffee and walnut cake is equally
tempting. On the tea front, guests have a
choice of five loose leaf teas – Ceylon,
Gunpowder Green, Darjeeling, Lapsang
Souchong and Assam – four herbal infusions
and two traditional teas. Add to all this the
tinkling of a piano or the strains of the
Pump Room Trio playing in the background
and your delightful afternoon tea is complete.

BERKSHIRE
MERCURE CASTLE HOTEL
Pennington Lounge and Windsor Bar
18 High Street, Windsor SL4 1LJ
Tel 01753 851577 (booking
recommended)
Fax 01753 830244
www.mercure-uk.com

Afternoon tea 3.00pm – 6.00pm (or any other time on request)
Two set teas Cream Tea, Traditional Full Afternoon Tea; à la carte menu also available
Location In town centre, opposite castle
Parking Private car park accessible from driveway down the side of the hotel
Places of interest nearby Windsor Castle, Eton College, Hampton Court, Runnymede, Windsor Great Park, Legoland, Dorney Court, Virginia Water, Theatre Royal, Savill Gardens, Thorpe Park
Groups welcome, but advance booking essential

The Mercure Castle Hotel, set right in the heart of historic Windsor, was built in 1528 as a coaching inn and was originally known as The Mermaid. It's a fine example of Georgian architecture and a refined place to take afternoon tea. The Pennington Lounge is a relaxing and comfortable room and has the additional benefit of giving one of the best vantage points to watch the splendid "Changing of the Guard" parade. You could arrive for morning coffee and view this spectacle, then perhaps visit Windsor Castle – the oldest royal residence to stay in constant use by monarchs of England – and then return later for tea.

Your afternoon tea is served in style – a three-tiered silver cake-stand laden with delicious finger sandwiches, scones, pastries and homely cake – accompanied by a pot of one of the usual teas. An exceptionally civilized experience.

CAMBRIDGESHIRE
THE ORCHARD TEA GARDENS
45–47 Mill Way, Grantchester,
Nr Cambridge CB3 9ND
Tel 01223 845788
Fax 01223 845862
e-mail otg@callan.co.uk
www.orchard-grantchester.com

Opening hours Daily all year, except some days over Christmas. Summer 9.30am – 5.30pm (but closing times vary); Winter 9.30am – 5.30pm
No set teas À la carte menu
Location The Orchard is situated on Mill Way, just below the church
Parking There is a large car park – but not large enough for coaches
Places of interest Cambridge city, punting on the river Granta, Rupert Brooke museum.

When the English poet, Rupert Brooke, wrote the lines "Stands the church clock at ten to three? And is there honey still for tea?" in the early 1900s, so ending one of his best-known poems *The Old Vicarage, Grantchester,* he immortalised afternoon tea in the Orchard. On a sunny summery day it is blissful to sit in a deck chair under the shade of an apple tree while you take tea. And on a winter's afternoon you can have a cosy seat in the Victorian Tea Pavilion set in the gardens of this old English orchard. Whatever the weather you get a real sense of time having been suspended – even though no one is certain whether the clock really did stop for Rupert Brooke. Apart from the extensive food menu, the afternoon tea offerings are equally traditional from the delights of home made fruit or plain scones, flapjacks, brownies and cookies to the quintessentially English Victoria Sponge or selection of other tempting cakes. Before you leave, take a stroll down to the river or wander around the orchard, and don't miss a visit to the Rupert Brooke museum.

CHESHIRE
KATIE'S TEA ROOMS
38 Watergate Street, Chester CH1 2LA
Tel 01244 400322
Fax 01244 400991
e-mail mito@fernan99.freeserve.co.uk

Opening hours Wednesday to Saturday 10.00am – 10.00pm; Sunday to Tuesday 10.00am – 5.00pm
Set afternoon tea and extensive tea à la carte menu
Wheelchair access Limited
Location Chester city centre; locate Chester Cross, follow Watergate Street leading from the Cross; shop is on right-hand side
Parking Public car parks nearby
Places of interest nearby Chester Roman City, Chester Cathedral, Chester Castle, Toy Museum, Chester Zoo

Silver teapots brimming with one of ten speciality leaf teas and three-tiered cake-stands laden with finger sandwiches, fruit scones and slices of cake, await you here in historic Chester. The black and white listed building is over 600 years old and has entrances from both street level and from the Chester Rows – through the magnificent original studded oak door – the galleried tiers of shops for which the medieval walled city is so famous. Inside these traditional tearooms, with their thick oak beams and original sandstone walls, all three floors are elegantly decorated, the ambience is warm and friendly and the staff are eager to please. After your delicious tea, why not take a gentle stroll around the city walls?

CORNWALL
ROSKILLY'S
The Croust House,
Tregellast Barton, St Keverne, Helston
TR12 6NX
Tel 01326 280479
Fax 01326 280320
e-mail admin@roskillys.co.uk
www.roskillys.co.uk

Opening hours Open daily from mid-
February 10.00am – 6.00pm. Winter
months, weekends only. Advisable to phone
for dates and times
One set tea Cornish Cream Tea; extensive
à la carte menu also available
Location From Helston, take Lizard Road;
turn left towards St Keverne at roundabout
at end of Culdrose airstation; after 14
kilometres (9 miles) take right-hand fork to
Coverack; follow brown signs
Parking Own car park
Places of interest nearby Working farm,
craft shop; surrounding countryside is
designated an area of outstanding
natural beauty

Two generations of the Roskilly family
run this working farm, where every single
aspect of the enterprise has been
undertaken by them. The Croust House,
as the delightful tearooms are known, was
created out of the old milking parlour and
calf pens. The organic Jersey herd has a
new parlour, converted from a redundant
Dutch barn and you can watch the cows
being milked at 4.30pm one afternoon

and over-indulge on the golden home-
made clotted cream, ice cream, truffles
and fudge the next! Rachel Roskilly's
kitchen turns out wonderful home-made
food all day – the quiches are especially
good, but tea is a must, even at 10.00am
if that's what you fancy! Apart from the
wonderful scones and cream, which are
served with home-made preserves, there
are three-layer cakes like coffee, cherry
and brandy and crunchy caramel, cookies
and tray bakes. Bagged teas include Earl
and Lady Grey, Indian and Lapsang
Souchong. A little off the beaten track,
but well worth the detour.

DE WYNNS TEA AND COFFEE HOUSE

55 Church Street,
Falmouth,
Cornwall TR11 3DS
Tel 01326 319259
e-mail infodewynns@yahoo.com
www.dewynns.co.uk

Opening hours Monday to Saturday 10.00am – 5.00pm (all year round). Closed Sundays. Check for bank holiday opening
Wheelchair access Limited
Places of interest Falmouth's Golden Beaches, The National Maritime Museum, Harbours and Shipyards, Pendennis Castle

What better place to have tea in this historic town than at de Wynns, an award winning Tea and Coffee House named after one of Falmouth's earliest entrepreneurs. The Grade II listed building has a history all of its own, for links can be traced back to the Steam Packet Service which began in Falmouth in 1688 and which, by 1827, had well over thirty ships regularly sailing from the port to deliver post as far afield as America and the West Indies. Now a comfortable and friendly tea place, the traditional furnishings are a reminder of times past. The owners are great supporters of local producers, so expect to be served with strawberry preserve made from local berries, clotted cream churned on a farm close by, and tea grown on the nearby Tregothnan Estate.

CUMBRIA
HAZELMERE CAFÉ AND BAKERY

1-2 Yewbarrow Terrace,
Grange-Over-Sands,
Cumbria LA11 6ED
Tel 01539 532972
e-mail hazelmeregrange@yahoo.co.uk
www.hazelmerecafe.co.uk

Opening hours Daily. Spring/summer 10.00am – 5.00pm; autumn/winter 10.00am – 4.30pm. Closed Christmas Day, Boxing Day, New Year's Day and sometimes several other days around Christmas. Please phone for specific dates
Two set teas Hazelmere Traditional Afternoon Tea, Cumbrian Cream tea; also à la carte menu available.
Location From A 590 take B277 to Grange-over-Sands. Pass the station and then take the first left off the mini roundabout. Hazelmere is the first two properties on the right.
Parking Public car park on Windermere Road, 100 yards away (2nd left at mini roundabout)
Wheelchair access Limited – please phone in advance
Special dietary requirements catered for
Places of interest nearby Holker Hall and Gardens, Beatrix Potter Gallery and Hill Top, South Lakes Wild Animal Park, Windermere Lake Cruises, Leighton Moss Nature Reserve, Levens Hall and Gardens
Children welcome High chairs and colouring sheets can be provided

There have been refreshments on offer at the Hazelmere since it first opened its doors to weary travellers in 1897. Situated in a delightful Victorian seaside resort on the English Lakes South Peninsula, the Grade II listed building is now home to this award-winning and most welcoming café. In the winter you can sit in front of a roaring log fire, in summer bask in the sun under the glass canopy. Everything is made on the premises from the highest quality ingredients, with special emphasis on local produce. There is Lakeland whipped cream to go with the white sultana or brown cherry scones, and home made jams – including, plum, gooseberry, blackcurrant and Lyth Valley damson – to complete the treat. On the cake side, Cumberland Rum Nicky takes some beating – the recipe for this house speciality originated from the Cumberland coast trade with the West Indies and is a delectable combination of dates, cherries, rum butter and ginger in a sweet pastry case. Or the faint hearted can opt for a delicious vanilla or ginger slice. Accompany whatever you eat with a leaf chosen from the extensive list, for Hazelmere is a tea lover's paradise: from the Special House Tea, through black teas from Sri Lanka, India, Malaysia, China and Africa to green teas from Japan, Sri Lanka, India and China to Oolongs and the more unusual Silver Tips White Tea and more…the selection is endless. You can also take the opportunity of trying three different teas with the Ceylonese Tea Taster's Tray – an unusual addition to a very special tea.

SHARROW BAY COUNTRY HOUSE HOTEL
Lake Restaurant
Lake Ullswater, Penrith CA10 2LZ
Tel 01768 486301 (booking essential for non-residents)
Fax 01768 486349
e-mail enquiries@sharrow-bay.com
www.sharrowbay.co.uk

Afternoon tea 4.00pm – 6.00pm
Set afternoon tea Fixed price
Location A592 to Pooley Bridge, turn right after church
Parking Hotel car park
Wheelchair access Limited – please phone in advance to enquire
Places of interest nearby Lake District National Park

The Sharrow Bay Hotel is a luxurious small hotel created over 50 years ago by an enterprising young man who was determined, against the odds, to make a personal dream come true. He fell in love with the stunning views of Lake Ullswater and the surrounding fells and the innumerable awards bestowed upon the hotel are a testimony to the great success of the venture.

Nothing about Sharrow Bay is understated: the décor is theatrical and sumptuous, there are wonderful fresh flowers everywhere and antiques and bric-à-brac are to be found in every corner. The ambience here is warm and welcoming, the service impeccable. Note that children under 13 years of age are not admitted at Sharrow Bay.

Don't have lunch beforehand, nor arrange to have another meal that day, for the assortment and quantity of delicacies served at tea are beyond your wildest imagination. Non-residents are served tea in the Lake Restaurant, seated at a table by the window. From this vantage point you can bask in the wonderful views whilst savouring delectable finger sandwiches, scones, teacakes and home-made cakes and pastries ranging from fruit cake, fruit tartlets, chocolate éclairs and iced lemon cake. The selection changes daily and what you don't manage to eat will be packed up in a box for you to take away and enjoy later. Your teapot, filled with Darjeeling, Lapsang Souchong, Keemun or other leaf tea will be kept warm under a delightful chintz tea cosy.

Location Just off A6, in the Market Square
Parking Public car parks in local area
Places of interest nearby Evening tours of the Pudding Shop; exploring the beautiful Peak District, 5 kilometres (3 miles) from Chatsworth and Haddon Hall

---

DERBYSHIRE
THE OLD ORIGINAL BAKEWELL PUDDING SHOP

The Square, Bakewell DE45 1BT
Tel 01629 812193
Fax 01629 812260
www.bakewellpuddingshop.co.uk

Opening hours May to October 9.00am – 9.00pm; November to April 9.00am – 5.00pm
Two set teas Bakewell Cream Tea, Full Afternoon Tea; tea à la carte also served
Wheelchair access None

One thing you won't get at the Old Original Bakewell Pudding Shop is the secret recipe for the all-time favourite Bakewell pudding. It has been hand-made in the kitchens of this charming seventeenth-century building for over 100 years and came about by accident, when, in the 1860s, a local cook spread strawberry jam over some pastry and then poured egg mixture over the top before cooking it. The result was an instant success and a Mrs Wilson managed to obtain the recipe and went into business making puddings. The rest is history.

Feast your eyes on the wonderful window display of larder goods as you enter the shop and have a look at the huge selection of cakes and breads before you climb the stairs to the bustling first-floor restaurant. Oak beams and antique copper kitchen paraphernalia add to the feeling of times past. Whether you have a traditional set tea or order à la carte, make sure you have a slice of Bakewell pudding, served as it should be – hot with custard or cream. Bagged teas on offer include Darjeeling and Ceylon. Before you leave, why not buy a pudding to take home?

DEVON
THE JOLLY ROGER TEAROOMS
6 Piazza Terracine, Haven Road, Exeter, Devon EX2 8GT
Tel 01392 433313

Opening hours Daily. March to October 9.00am – 5.30pm; November to February 10.00am – 5.00pm
Two set teas Jolly Roger Tea, Cream Tea; full à la carte menu also available
Wheelchair access
Location Follow signs for Exeter Quay
Parking No parking in immediate area
Places of interest nearby Within the Exeter Quay and Canal Trust; tearooms are overlooking historic canal basin
Most dietary requirements can be met

There is a lovely homely feeling about the Jolly Roger Tearoom, which occupies an enviable position on the historic Exeter Quay. It's light and airy but warm and cosy and is furnished with an eclectic mix of old and new furniture. There is a distinctively nautical jaunt about the place, and fresh flowers abound both inside and out, where on a good day you can sit in comfort under a glazed canopy, shielded from the sun by a huge umbrella. The selection of home made cakes and scones is vast, and always has a seasonal note – you might find strawberry or chocolate scones on the menu alongside the ever present plain, sultana and apple ones. Don't forget to try the apple and ginger jam. All-time favourite cakes include carrot, orange and lemon drizzle, as well as coffee and walnut, but there is always a surprise in store and something special on offer. Tea drinking is very much part of the whole experience and the selection of loose teas is astonishing – over one hundred varieties. This really is afternoon tea as it used to be.

DORSET
THE OLD TEA HOUSE
44 High West Street, Dorchester DT1 1UT
Tel 01305 263719

Opening hours June to October 10.00am – 5.00pm; November to May 10.00am – 4.00pm; closed Mondays and all through January
One set tea Dorset Cream Tea or tea à la carte
Wheelchair access
Location In the centre of town, on the main street, near Top-o-Town roundabout
Parking Public car park 50 metres (55 yards) away

Places of interest nearby Devon and Dorset Military Museum, Roman Town House, Thomas Hardy memorabilia in Dorset County Museum
No high chairs, and limited access for buggies

There has been a tearoom here since 1902, but the picturesque, white-washed building, with its bay windows and striped awnings, dates back to 1635. Inside is just what you would hope to find in a quintessentially English tearoom – inglenook fireplace, original beams, working gas lights and a warm, welcoming atmosphere.

The Dorset Cream Tea is a favourite, choose one of four types of scones – plain,

fruit, wholemeal and cheese. Don't miss the "naughty but nice" speciality Dorset Apple Cake – sponge, a layer of apple topped with crumble and served warm with clotted cream or ice cream to go with your beverage – the standard range is on offer here. The Old Tea House is unable to cater for special dietary requirements.

GLOUCESTERSHIRE
LORDS OF THE MANOR
Upper Slaughter, near Bourton-on-the Water, GL54 2JD
Tel 01451 820243
Fax 01451 820696
e-mail enquiries@lordsofthemanor.com
www.lordsofthemanor.com

Opening hours Monday to Saturday 3.30pm – 5.30pm; Sunday 4.00pm – 5.30pm
Two set teas Cream Tea, Full Afternoon Tea; also tea and biscuits
Location Take A429 towards Stow-on-the Wold then turn towards The Slaughters and Lower Slaughter
Parking Hotel has own car park
Places of interest nearby Bourton-on-the Water, the Cotswolds, Kiftsgate and Hidcote Gardens, Sudeley Castle, Warwick Castle, Blenheim Palace

The poet Milton is reputed to have written his famous trilogy Paradise Lost at Eyford, just 1 kilometre (½ mile) upstream of Slaughter Brook, which meanders through

The Old Tea House

the delightful grounds of the Lords of the Manor. The honey-coloured Cotswold stone house was once a rectory and parts of it date back to 1650. Inside, comfortable sofas, real fires, handsome antiques and family portraits add to the warm convivial atmosphere of a fine country house and it is a most agreeable place to enjoy a traditional afternoon tea.

There's a lovely terrace where you can take tea, weather permitting, or try one of the lounges, the drawing-room or bar. Whichever place you choose you'll be served graciously. It's all linen cloths and napkins, silver tea-ware and tiered cake-stands and you will drool over the very fresh scones, prepared to Ma Rennie's own recipe – she is the Executive Chef's mother – and then you can indulge in a slice of home-made cake from the day's selection. Seasonal changes might present you with elderflower jelly for the scones, or some additional flower teas in the summer. Otherwise you could just settle for homemade biscuits and a cup of tea from the 15 varieties of loose leaf on offer.

NOTTINGHAMSHIRE
OLLERTON WATERMILL TEASHOP

Market Place, Ollerton, Newark
NG22 9AA
Tel 01623 822469

Opening hours Open from the end of
March to mid November, Wednesday to
Sunday 10.30am – 4.00pm. Bookings
encouraged for lunchtime. No tea bookings
taken though.
One set tea Ollerton Mill Cream Tea;
tea à la carte also available
Wheelchair access Limited as the teashop
is situated upstairs, but there is a small
foyer table for two to three people on the
ground floor
Location Ollerton lies at the junction of
the A614 and B616, between Worksop and
Nottingham; the Watermill is almost
opposite the church
Parking In public village car park
Places of interest nearby Nottingham,
Sherwood Forest, Ollerton Mill exhibition

Situated on the edge of Sherwood Forest is
a tiny corner of rural England where you'll
find the unspoilt village of Ollerton and
where not much has changed for three
centuries. There has been a mill on the spot
since 1713 and its fascinating history gives
visitors a peek at what life was like for a
working miller in the eighteenth century.
The ground floor of the red brick building
boasts a 5-metre (16-foot) diameter
waterwheel, dating from 1862 and Kate
and Ellen Mettam's award-winning

teashop is housed upstairs in the old
millwright's workshop.

You get a splendid view of the mill race
and waterwheel from the entrance and of
the River Maun from the teashop. Simple
furnishings – white-topped pine tables, pine
chairs and whitewashed walls – complete
the tranquil setting for a tea which is a truly
old-fashioned event and a real treat.
Delectable home-made food is the order of
the day and as you might expect, the mill –
restored and run by the Mettam husbands –
produces all the finest milled flour used in
the baking. Traditional scones – plain,
cheese or wholemeal fruit – emerge from
the ovens at regular intervals. Generous
slices of wholesome cakes, including coffee
and walnut, lemon and the very popular
carrot cake are served. There's Bakewell tart
or, for the totally indulgent, pavlova filled
with fresh cream and fruit. Regular visitors
are used to having their tea-tasting buds
challenged by the "guest teas" which appear
on the menu from time to time, but there is
always a wide variety of bagged teas
available, including Lapsang Souchong,
Lady Grey and Assam available.

No visit for tea would be complete without a look at the exhibition which tells the story of Ollerton Mill from Doomsday England to the present day – truly living history. And if you are a home baker, then why not buy some Ollerton Mill flour on your way out?

OXFORDSHIRE
OLD PARSONAGE HOTEL
Parsonage Bar
1 Banbury Road, Oxford OX2 6NN
Tel 01865 292305 (bookings always advisable, and essential during graduation time)
Fax 01865 311262
e-mail reception@oldparsonage-hotel.co.uk
www.oldparsonage-hotel.co.uk

Opening hours Monday to Thursday 3.00pm – 5.30pm; Friday and Saturday 3.00pm – 5.00pm; Sunday 3.30pm – 5.30pm
Three set teas Very High Tea, Graduation Tea, Light Tea; tea à la carte also available
Wheelchair access Wheelchair access by prior arrangement
Location On Banbury Road, at north end of St Giles, next to St Giles Church; between Somerville and Keble Colleges
Parking Hotel has private car park
Places of interest nearby Colleges of Oxford University, punting on River Cherwell, Ashmolean Museum

A favourite with parents reviving the flagging spirits of their student offspring or hungry school children, the Old Parsonage has a well-deserved reputation for serving a very good, old-fashioned afternoon tea. The

creeper-clad, honey-stoned seventeenth-century building has a remarkably colourful history. It has served as a safe haven for persecuted clergy, been a stronghold for Royalists and was even home to Oscar Wilde. The sense of the past is still evident inside, even though the hotel has been modernized. Old features have been retained and the ambience is that of a smart townhouse with panelling, comfortable leather chairs and walls covered in old prints. There is a delightful front terrace where you can enjoy tea, weather permitting.

Everything from the sandwiches to the scones – plain or cheese – to the cakes is home-baked and delicious. Quality leaf teas served in china pots include Lapsang Souchong, Darjeeling and the house Old Parsonage Blend. Owner Jeremy Mogford's philosophy is to give you the best and his staff ensure you have a wonderful time and enjoy a real treat.

EAST SUSSEX
MOCK TURTLE TEA-SHOP
4 Pool Valley, Brighton BN1 1NJ
Tel 01273 327380

Opening hours Tuesday to Sunday 9.30am – 6.30pm; closed Mondays. Closed from 23 December until 3 January
Set cream tea and huge à la carte menu
Wheelchair access Two steps into shop, limited space inside
Location Very near to The Lanes and The Royal Pavilion

Parking Voucher, meter and public car parks in town centre
Places of interest nearby The Lanes, Royal Pavilion, sea front
Children welcome, but no high chairs
No debit or credit cards taken

The Mock Turtle is really a country teashop in town and it has a very traditional feel about it. Whether you have just marvelled at the splendour of the Royal Pavilion, browsed through the antique shops in the nearby Lanes or had a bracing walk along the promenade and pier, the irresistible food served here will revive and restore you. The owners pride themselves on using only the freshest, highest quality ingredients, including locally-produced honey and cream. Everything, from the bread to the florentines and flapjacks, is prepared on the premises, often to their own recipes. Choose either fluffy white or wholemeal scones, topped with butter, whipped cream and jam followed by one of the Mock Turtle's famous melt-in-the-mouth meringues filled with (more) cream and fresh seasonal fruit. There is a wide range of the finest loose leaf teas. Wholesome, homely and heavenly.

WEST SUSSEX
SHEPHERDS TEA ROOMS
35 Little London, Chichester PO19 2PL
Tel/Fax 01243 774761

Opening hours Monday to Friday 9.15am – 5.00pm; Saturday 9.00am – 5.00pm; Sunday 10.00am – 4.00pm. Closed all bank holidays.
Two set afternoon teas Shepherds Cream Tea, Traditional Cream Tea; extensive tea à la carte menu
Wheelchair access None
Location In city centre; Little London just off East Street
Parking Public car parks nearby
Places of interest nearby Goodwood House and Racecourse, South Downs, Chichester and harbour, Chichester Festival Theatre

Inside the lovely listed Georgian building off Chichester's busy high street is Shepherds. Oak floors, airy lemon and pale lime décor and personal service add to the calm atmosphere in which you can feast on an award-winning traditional tea and drink a very invigorating beverage.

You won't be able to resist the mouth-watering home-made scones – either fruit, cheese or wholemeal. Then there are the hearty, wholesome cakes like the very popular Earl Grey tea-bread, orange and sultana slices or coffee and walnut cake.

Frankly, you'll be spoilt for choice by the tempting display in the teashop. And if you are feeling quite hungry, then a savoury option of rarebit, the speciality of the house, is an absolute must. The biggest problem is deciding which of the six unusual variations – maybe Stilton and Tomato or Hawaiian – to order. There's the usual range of leaf teas, as well as Pure Assam and some green teas. A very "English" tea indeed, in a quintessentially English teashop.

WARWICKSHIRE
BENSONS
4 Bard's Walk, Stratford-upon-Avon
CV37 6EY
Tel 01789 261116
www.bensonsrestaurant.co.uk

Opening hours Monday to Friday 9.00am – 5.30pm; Saturday 8.30am – 5.30pm; Sunday 10.30am – 5.00pm
Two set afternoon teas Full Traditional, Champagne Tea; tea à la carte menu also
Location Two minutes walk from Shakespeare's Birthplace on Henley Street, opposite main post office
Parking Public car parks in town centre
Places of interest nearby Shakespeare's birthplace, Anne Hathaway's Cottage, Swan Theatre

From the outside of Bensons, with its restored nineteenth-century façade, you might expect to find a quaint, old-fashioned tearoom. Instead, you are treated to a light and airy contemporary conservatory-style interior, abundant with flowers, foliage and original watercolours. The calm and relaxing ambience is wonderful and a complete contrast to the busy world outside. And all this before you have sampled the gourmet tea!

Bensons works closely with the internationally renowned Maison Blanc, originally established by leading chef, Raymond Blanc and the daily changing selection of hand-made patisserie on offer is simply divine. Just imagine Millefeuille Framboise – layers of caramelized pâte feuilletée with crème mousseline and fresh raspberries – and you'll know what I mean! For the less adventurous, the traditional afternoon tea of freshly prepared sandwiches, warm scones with clotted cream and conserves will not fail to please. Extra special is the Champagne Tea, for you are served a half-bottle of fine, chilled house bubbly alongside the tea sandwiches, scones, afternoon pastries and traditional fruit cake. The quality and presentation of food at Bensons is exemplary and it has to be one of Stratford-upon-Avon's best kept secrets. It comes as no surprise that it is a multi award-winner.

Opening hours Monday to Saturday 9.30am – 9.00pm; Sunday 11.00am – 8.30pm. Closed Christmas Day and Boxing Day

Four set teas The Bridge Cream Tea, The Bridge Full Afternoon Tea, Victorian Afternoon Tea, Masters and Mistresses Afternoon Tea

Location Near public library on St Margaret's Street side of bridge

Parking Public car park by tearooms

Places of interest nearby Saxon church, fourteenth-century tithe barn, Bath, Great Chalfield Manor (National Trust), Corsham Court, Wiltshire countryside

---

WILTSHIRE
THE BRIDGE TEA ROOMS
24A Bridge Street, Bradford-on-Avon
BA15 1BY
Tel 01225 865537

This award-winning tearoom, originally built in 1675 as a blacksmith's cottage, oozes character with its tiny windows and low entrance. Hanging baskets and window boxes are a blaze of colour in the summer. The interior is a bit of a surprise, for it is reminiscent of the Victorian age, complete with the aspidistra plant, commemorative china and a picture of the great Queen herself gazing down on you from the wall. The friendly staff, in their starched uniforms, could easily have walked out of the original ABC teashop on London Bridge. Add to this the delightful views of the thirteenth-century town bridge and you know that you are in for a treat.

All the set teas include the essential ingredients – scones, jam and Devonshire clotted cream – but you can also include sandwiches and mini pastries if the mood takes you. You can add a glass of champagne for a special celebration, and choose from a selection of delicious homely cakes and mouth-watering meringue creations. For those who prefer, there is Savoury Afternoon Tea, which features cheese scones, and a special menu for children. All the tea served here is loose leaf and of the finest quality and the discerning tea drinker will find some 28 to choose from, including Ceylon Silver Tip, Pai-Mutan China White, First Flush Darjeeling, and Nilgri Broken Orange Pekoe.

Wheelchair access
Location In Broadway High Street, overlooking The Green and the War Memorial
Parking Public car park 180 metres (200 yards) through arcade at rear of shop
Places of interest nearby Broadway, Snowshill Manor, Hidcote Manor, Sudeley Castle, Cotswolds
No debit or credit cards
High chair available

Here is a traditional teashop right in the heart of one of the Cotswolds' most popular villages. The warm sandstone building, at the lower end of Broadway High Street opposite the War Memorial, dates from the 17th century and has an old world charm all of its own. Quintessentially English, there is an old fashioned bicycle with delivery basket propped up outside the door and a bow-fronted window with its display of tea paraphernalia.

Taking tea here is a really serious business.

WORCESTERSHIRE
TISANES
Cotswold House, 21 The Green, Broadway WR12 7AA
Tel 01386 853296
e-mail infor@tisanes-tearooms.co.uk
www.tisanes-tearooms.co.uk

Opening hours Daily 10.00am – 5.00pm except Christmas Day
Tea à la carte

The list of more than 30 teas and herbal and fruit infusions means that there is something to please every palate. Rwanda Burundi, Darjeeling Vintage and Formosa Oolong are on the regular list, and there is always a special "tea of the week" available. Nor will the food on offer disappoint in any way. There are plain and fruit scones, teacakes and toast, and wholesome cakes like Victoria Sponge, Carrot or Chocolate Fudge, and the house speciality, Coffee and Walnut, as well as a surprise "guest cake". 1930s and 40s music is played in the shop, and your visit may not be complete without making a musical purchase before you leave. Or you might prefer to buy a jar of jam or honey from the Elizabethan England range of products which are based on genuine 16th century stillroom recipes.

YORKSHIRE
BETTYS CAFÉ TEAROOMS
1 Parliament Street, Harrogate HG1 2QU
Tel 01423 877300
Fax 01423 877307
Opening hours 9.00am – 9.00pm
www.bettysandtaylors.com
www.bettysbypost.com

Two set afternoon teas Bettys Traditional, Cream Tea; extensive tea à la carte menu
Location Bettys is situated in the town centre on the main Leeds to Ripon route; the tearooms stand at the very top of Montpelier Hill
Parking Metered parking available locally

Places of interest nearby Old Pump Rooms, Turkish Baths, Harlow Carr Botanical Gardens, gateway to the Dales

Lady Raine Spencer once drooled over Bettys, praising it as better than any of the hundreds of teashops she and her husband had visited in cities all over the world. Few could disagree with this sentiment for Bettys has earned a worldwide reputation for excellence since it was founded in Harrogate, in 1919, by an adventurous and talented Swiss ancestor of the present owners. The Harrogate teashop, with its art deco mirrors, panelling, oak staircase and picture windows overlooking Montpelier Gardens and The Stray, is an oasis of calm and elegance and is on any tourist's list of places to visit. Like all of the six branches, it is the very epitome of Yorkshire warmth and hospitality.

Of all the delicious food served at Bettys it's the Yorkshire Fat Rascal that is the most famous – so much so that it has its own range of products, including pottery mugs and teapots. Just thinking about this rich fruity scone, made with citrus peel, almonds and cherries, makes my taste buds tingle. Bettys Craft Bakery is the creative heart of the business and everything, from the pikelets (a Yorkshire crumpet) and tea-loaves to the amazing array of cakes and patisserie is hand-baked there. You can see how the Swiss Alps meets the Yorkshire Dales with the choice between a super rich Swiss Chocolate Torte and a traditional Yorkshire Curd Tart. You are truly spoilt for choice.

The tea served at Bettys comes from their sister company, the renowned tea merchants, Taylors of Harrogate. Order either of the two set teas and you'll be served the excellent Tea Room Blend Tea, but for the aficionado there are speciality teas to dream about. Ceylon Blue Sapphire, Special Estate Darjeeling or Tippy Assam as well as China Rose Petal and "Good Luck" Green Tea are on the list and these and many more are on sale in the shop – along with the Fat Rascal pottery mugs! There are also four other branches of Bettys, details of which below.

BETTYS CAFÉ TEAROOMS
32 The Grove, Ilkley LS29 9EE
Tel 01943 608029
Opening hours Daily 9.00am – 5.30pm

BETTYS AT RHS GARDENS
Harlow Carr, Crag Lane, Beckwithshaw, Harrogate HG3 1QB
Tel 01423 505604
Opening hours Daily 9.00am – 5.30pm (5.00pm in winter)

BETTYS CAFÉ TEAROOMS
High Street, Northallerton DL7 8LF
Tel 01609 775154
Opening hours Monday to Saturday 9.00am – 5.30pm; Sunday 10.00am – 5.30pm

BETTYS CAFÉ TEAROOMS
6–8 St. Helen's Square, York YO1 8QP
Tel 01904 659142
Opening hours Daily 9.00am – 9.00pm

LITTLE BETTYS
46 Stonegate, York YO1 2AS
Tel 01904 622865
Opening hours Saturday 9.00am–5.30pm;
Sunday to Friday 10.00am–5.30pm

TREASURER'S HOUSE TEA ROOMS
Minster Yard, York YO1 7JL
Tel 01904 685565
e-mail
treasurershouse@nationaltrust.org.uk
www.nationaltrust.co.uk

Opening hours Monday to Thursday
11.00am – 4.30pm
Three set teas Cream Tea, House Party
Tea, Butler's Tea; tea à la carte menu
Wheelchair access Limited, but
refreshments can be served on the ground
floor by request
Location Signposted around York Minster
Parking City centre car parks
Places of interest nearby York City Art
Gallery, York Minster, Jorvik Viking
Centre, National Railway Museum,
Museum Gardens, Barley Hall

You may be "below stairs" here, ensconced
in that intriguing part of every grand house
which was inhabited by an army of
servants, but you certainly get a true sense
of the history of the splendid Treasurers
House by being here. Set in the shadow of
York Minster, the last owner of the house
was an Edwardian gentleman by the name
of Frank Green, who was passionate about

good food. He would undoubtedly have
approved of the cosy and welcoming
atmosphere of the National Trust tearooms
which visitors flock to for its home-baking.
The Yorkshire curd tart and lemon curd
tart make your tongue tingle and the
toasted crumpets served with the Butler's
tea drip with melting butter. The
Housekeeper's tea has a real Northern feel,
for it features parkin, the traditional
favourite made with oatmeal and treacle,
served with Yorkshire cheese and fruit. And
what better than a strong cup of Yorkshire
tea to complete the treat?

SCOTLAND
FIFE
KIND KYTTOCK'S KITCHEN
Cross Wynd, Falkland KY15 7BE
Tel 01337 857477

Afternoon tea available all day
Two set teas Cream Tea, Afternoon Tea;
large à la carte menu
Wheelchair access Ground floor only –
advance notice appreciated
Location At the centre of Falkland near the
palace, turn up at the square into Cross Wynd
Parking On-street parking opposite
Places of interest nearby Falkland Palace,
Garden and Old Burgh

Kind Kyttock was a woman who, legend
has it, served food to weary travellers
passing through the area. The
establishment named after her is so popular

MIDLOTHIAN
THE BALMORAL
The Drawing Room, 1 Princes Street, Edinburgh EH2 2EQ, Scotland
Tel 0131 556 2414 (for tea bookings, which are strongly recommended, and essential during the Edinburgh festival)
Fax 0131 557 3747
www.thebalmoralhotel.com

Opening hours 12.00noon – 5.00pm
Set tea The Balmoral Tea, with or without a glass of Bollinger Special Cuvée or Moët & Chandon Brut Rosé
Location Princes Street, next to Waverley Station
Places of interest nearby Edinburgh Castle, Palace of Holyrood House, The Royal Mile, Edinburgh Zoo, Royal Yacht Britannia, Royal Botanic Garden, Scotch

with locals and visitors that if you arrive later than 10.45am on a Sunday morning, you'll be hard pushed to find a table. Sandwiched in the middle of an early eighteenth century terrace, the interior is cosy and comforting, especially when the open fire is roaring on a cold winter's day. Dark furniture and bright tablecloths add to the charming traditional feel. Whatever you choose from the menu, be it the scones or Scot's pancakes (drop scones), the deliciously sweet Campbell Fudge Cake, date shortbread or any of the other delectable items on offer, the homely food will leave a lingering impression. You'll be served an excellent brew of leaf tea from the range on offer which includes Golden Ceylon, Pure China and Russian. It's no wonder that this lovely teashop has won so many awards.

Whisky Heritage Centre. The Balmoral is also close to many of the leading luxury department stores.

While many Edinburgh hotels claim to have Edinburgh's landmarks on their doorstep, few can say their doorstep is a landmark. Set in the very heart of Edinburgh and overlooking Edinburgh Castle, there has been an hotel on the site since 1902, following W. Hamilton Beattie and A.R. Scott's competition success to build the North British Station Hotel. Things have moved on since then and Rocco Forte's The Balmoral, with its majestic clock tower (and clock which still runs 3 minutes early so you don't miss your train), is now a luxury hotel in the true sense of the word. Take tea in either the Palm Court or the comfortable and relaxing Drawing Room with its views of Princes Street and you will feast on the finest finger sandwiches on Oatmeal or Malted Brown Bread, and enjoy a heavenly selection of home made scones – for example, Fruit, Heather Honey and mini chocolate – all served with preserves and Devon clotted cream. In true Scottish tradition there is Balmoral shortbread and Dundee cake to follow. Loose leaf teas include Royal Scottish Balmoral Blend, Famous Edinburgh and the glamorous Silver Needle. If you are visiting during the Edinburgh Festival, when the demand for afternoon tea is especially high, extra space is made available to accommodate more guests, so no one need miss out.

CLARINDA'S TEAROOM

69 Canongate, Royal Mile, Edinburgh
EH8 8BT
Tel 0131 557 1888

Opening hours Monday to Saturday
8.30am – 4.45pm; Sunday 9.30am –
4.45pm
Tea à la carte
No wheelchair access
Location On the Royal Mile
Places of interest nearby Palace of
Holyrood House, Scottish Parliament
Building, People's Museum, Edinburgh
Museum

The story goes that Clarinda (Agnes
Maclehose 1759–1841) was a friend and
mentor to Robert Burns, Scotland's most
famous poet, and was the inspiration for
his popular love song Ae Fond Kiss. The
teashop named after her is very traditional
inside – all lace tablecloths and Victorian
bric-a-brac, some of which is for sale. Note
that there is limited space for pushchairs
and no high chairs are available.

Excellent home-cooked food emerges
from the kitchen here and you'll be served
very traditional teatime treats including
scones and cream, rock cakes, banana
bread and other favourites. The day's
selection is displayed on the wooden
trolley for you to choose from. The leaf tea
available includes Scottish Breakfast and
Japanese Green. For sheer value for money,
Clarinda's is very hard to beat and is a very
cosy place to take tea.

STRATHCLYDE
THE WILLOW TEA ROOMS

217 Sauchiehall Street, Glasgow G2 3EX
Tel/Fax 0141 332 0521
e-mail
sauchiehallstreet@willowtearooms.co.uk
www.willowtearooms.co.uk

Also at: *97 Buchanan Street, Glasgow*
G1 3HF
Tel 0141 204 5242
e-mail
buchananstreet@willowtearooms.co.uk

Opening hours Monday to Saturday
9.00am – 5.00pm (last orders 4.30pm);
Sunday 11.00am – 4.15pm (last orders
3.45pm). Closed Christmas Day and New
Year's Day.
Two set teas Cream Tea, Afternoon Tea;
huge tea à la carte menu
No wheelchair access (tearoom on first
floor)
Location Centre of Glasgow
Parking Public car parks nearby
Places of interest nearby Burrell
Collection, Scotland Street School
Museum, Glasgow School of Art,
Hunterian Art Gallery

You really are stepping back in time to the
early 1900s when you take tea at the
Willow Tea Rooms, for this art nouveau
treasure is a wondrous recreation of the
original which Charles Rennie Mackintosh,
the famed architect and artist, designed and
built for his client, Kate Cranston, in 1903.

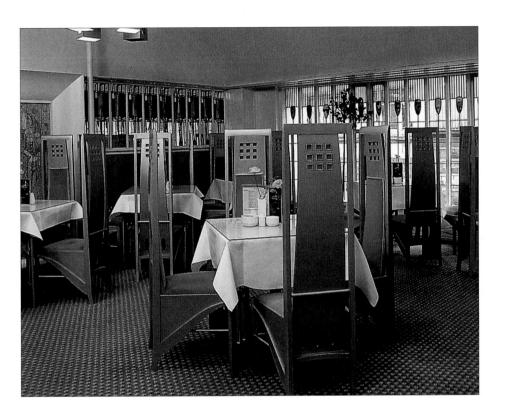

Now, as then, the main attraction, other than the glorious food, is the Room de Luxe, resplendent with silver furniture and leaded mirror friezes, much of which was rescued from the dismantled shop after it closed in 1928. The chairs, tables and lights have all been recreated to the original designs. Anne Mulhern, the proprietress, has certainly managed to capture the feeling of a bygone age, for the pace here is unhurried and the service superior.

There is such an extensive menu that you can eat all day long if you want, with lots of Scottish savoury dishes to choose from. All the old favourite traditional tea food is here, and amongst the array of cakes and pastries are Sinful Chocolate Slice, which rather speaks for itself, and Empire biscuit, a double layer of shortbread sandwiched with jam and dusted with icing sugar. Anne's own massive chewy meringues are amazing and by far the most popular treat. When it comes to tea, the beverage list is extensive and includes Gunpowder Green and Russian Caravan, as well as a total of 13 herbal and fruit teas. Taking tea here is a unique experience and one not to be missed. A range of souvenirs are available to buy including prints of the exterior of the building, fine bone china mugs and bags or caddies of tea.

WALES
GLAMORGAN
THE MUSEUM OF WELSH LIFE
Gwalia Tea Rooms
St Fagans, Cardiff CF5 6XB
Tel/Fax 029 2056 6985

Opening hours 10.00am – 4.00pm except Christmas day, Boxing Day and New Years Day
One set tea and extensive à la carte menu
Location Exit 33 off M4, follow signs to the Museum of Welsh Life; tearooms are in grounds of museum (free admission to museum)
Parking Museum car park
Places of interest nearby Cardiff Castle, Cardiff Bay, Brecon Beacons

Traditional home-made Welsh teatime treats such as bara brith, teisen lap and Welsh cakes all appear on the menu of the glorious Gwalia Tea Rooms, set within the grounds of Cardiff's Museum of Welsh Life. Taking tea in this delightful establishment is to step back in time to the art deco period of the 1920s, for the tearoom is on the first floor of the Gwalia Stores, a local department store which has been reconstructed, stone by stone, within the museum. Traditional afternoon tea here includes dainty sandwiches, a Welsh cake and a warm scone, but you can always go à la carte and tuck into a slightly spiced and fruity Gwalia rock cake or a custard slice, another favourite on the menu. You've an extensive choice of some

40 leaf teas, including Oolong, Yunnan, Gunpowder and Rose Pouchong.

In case you are wondering, bara brith is a traditional Welsh fruit-bread, that has a heavy mixed fruit content and a fine blend of mixed spices. Welsh cakes are small and pastry-based, made to a traditional recipe of currants and mixed spices, lightly toasted on a griddle. Teisen lap means "cake plate" and is a slice of lightly fruited sponge cake which has been cooked on a plate rather than in a tin. Mike Morton can arrange to send you some Welsh cakes or bara brith if you find yourself suffering from withdrawal symptoms.

LLANDUDNO
ST TUDNO HOTEL
North Parade, Promenade,
Llandudno LL30 2LP
Tel 01492 874411
Fax 01492 860407
e-mail sttudnohotel@btinternet.co.uk
www.st-tudno.co.uk

Afternoon tea 2.30pm – 5.30pm
Two set teas Welsh Afternoon Tea, De Luxe Afternoon Tea
Wheelchair access Limited
Location On the promenade, opposite the pier entrance and gardens
Parking Hotel car park
Places of interest nearby Conwy and Caernarfon Castle, Budnant Gardens, Snowdonia National Park, Anglesey

There is something very special about taking tea at St Tudno's. This seaside hotel and its afternoon tea, have received heaps of awards and once you have sampled the warm hospitality, comfort and luxury you'll understand why. It doesn't matter whether you are cosily settled in the sitting room with its delightful views of the seafront, ensconced in one of the comfortable lounges or watching the world go by from the front terrace, your tea will be served in style. Fine Wedgwood china, crisp linen tablecloths and napkins add to the feeling of quiet refinement.

The set teas combine tradition – sandwiches, scones with cream and jam and cake – with the local specialities of bara brith and Welsh cakes. Generous slices of coffee and walnut, Victoria sponge or chocolate fudge are just some of the cakes served with tea. The De Luxe tea includes all of this plus smoked salmon, strawberries and cream and a glass of champagne and it is quite a struggle to get through all of the delicious home-made food.

The quality and selection of teas is equally impressive, with some 17 varieties to choose from. The attention to detail here is most impressive – from the silver, tiered cake-stands to the choice of skimmed, semi-skimmed or whole milk for your tea.

Picture Credits

Index